*To
God loves you.
Bill Waters*

The Gospel of Bill

by

Just Bill

Just Bill

See, I Have Engraved You on the Palms of My Hands

DORRANCE PUBLISHING CO., INC.
PITTSBURGH, PENNSYLVANIA 15222

All Rights Reserved
Copyright © 2010 by Just Bill
No part of this book may be reproduced or transmitted
in any form or by any means, electronic or mechanical,
including photocopying, recording, or by any information
storage and retrieval system without permission in
writing from the publisher.

ISBN: 978-1-4349-0553-6
Printed in the United States of America

First Printing

For more information or to order additional books, please contact:
Dorrance Publishing Co., Inc.
701 Smithfield Street
Pittsburgh, Pennsylvania 15222
U.S.A.
1-800-788-7654
www.dorrancebookstore.com

I dedicate this book to my immediate family who lived through this monumental Spiritual Event with me.

I also dedicate this book to millions of aborted babies throughout the world

Foreword

The Gospel is the GOOD NEWS of HOW TO BE SAVED. While the gospel is good news, it has the heart, a tragedy of the birth and death of Christ who died for our sins. GOD was able to use this event in the most welcomed news we have ever received. Jesus was betrayed and arrested. He was bound by his enemies and forsaken by his disciples. Jesus was tried and wrongfully convicted of blasphemy which was punishable by death in the Jewish system. His stripes were visible front and back, upper and lower, and His blood poured out profusely from the whippings he sustained. He was spit upon and hit in the mouth, and who knows what else. By the time he was raised on the cross, he was a pitiful site to behold, yet this was indeed THE KING OF KINGS AND THE LORD OF LORDS for all people, for all times, suffering for us all by giving us HIS ALL. Amen!

Acknowledgements

I thank Father T., Father D. W., Dr. S, Dr. T, and JAO who helped me along the way, trying to keep me on an even keel.

Finally, I acknowledge everything I have written to be true to the best of my knowledge and in accordance with the Lord and his will.

Introduction

God loves you and me. No one loves us more than God, whether we are good or evil. In his eyes, we are unique and special for God doesn't make trash.

There is no other person just like you and me throughout the history of the world. Out of love for us, God made each one of us with the sole purpose for us to get to heaven.

God is good. He provides us with a worldly family to love and nurture us along the way. God wants us to know, love, and serve him, and believe in him and follow him to his Kingdom of Heaven when our lives end and a new life begins without end. Amen!

Sometimes, God uses nature to express himself to us but we have to be in tune with him by giving God as much quality time in prayer that we can.

God Almighty and Jesus both gave their entire selves to us when Jesus died on the cross for us, to save us from our sins.

Love God with all your heart, with all your soul, and with all your mind.

God wants us to get to heaven where he is waiting to welcome each one of us into his heavenly home.

This true story is about the supreme trials and blessings God showered on me—a poor sinner.

GOD'S WATCHFUL EYE

MAY BE LOOKING AT YOU AND I

Chapter One

Growing Up

I was born in 1943. If abortions were legal then, I would not be sharing this true story with you for I would have probably been aborted. I weighed only three pounds, making me a miracle baby I suppose. My parents had given me up for adoption at birth. I was very lucky for I was adopted by two wonderful parents, who lived in a little seaport town called Galveston in Texas. My adoptive mother rode a train by herself to Austin, Texas, to adopt a little girl. When she got to the Home of the Holy Infancy to adopt, they told her the little girl was very sick and could not be adopted. They brought her into a room full of little bitty babies and said I stood out for I was the only one smiling from ear-to-ear at her. I must have said, "Take me, I'm yours." She even had to go to court to finalize the adoption and sleep overnight in a hotel by herself. She did all this for me, ooh, lucky me. Well, that did it and I was on my way to Galveston. When my father saw me for the first time, he said, "But she has a tassel." It was great down by the sea; oh, how lucky I was to be me. I went to the beach and when I first saw it, my eyes became wide and my breath was taken away. The sea was so beautiful to me.

My great uncle and my father loved seeing me growing up. Unk, as we called him, was practically deaf and we had to holler in his ear for him to hear us. He went to the Catholic Church every day until he could no more. He loved to make duck decoys for those who liked to hunt ducks. He even called the ducks in the City Park for them to greet him. They came like the wind and we fed them. My father also liked to hunt ducks and geese and we hunted as often as we could until the season ended. I'll never forget the times I had with him at the run down hunting camp. As soon as the lights went out, the field mice came inside to get out of the cold weather. They pattered as they moved about on the floor, making scary noises. I had to sleep on the top bunk with the rafters just inches away from my face, and all I could do was worry the mice would climb on the rafters and jump on my face. I never slept very much because it was very scary there, with the mice and the snoring of other men that kept me awake all night. By 4:00 A.M. in the morning, the alarm would go off and I would say Amen, and jumped out of bed to dress for the coldest mornings I felt on earth. I fixed them a good breakfast and away we went to the duck blinds to hunt for them. It was so fine in the wintertime to draw a bead on an incoming duck with its wings locked in flight, ready to land.

My father also took me fishing nearly every spring and summer weekend, and we caught quite a few. My mother also liked to fish as often as she could, and it was a good outing for my family. My father also took me to his college school's Saturday night football games in Houston, Texas, and I would yell and scream at the top of my lungs for his team to win in the end. Those were the days, and I was so lucky to have had such great parents who liked doing things with me all of the time.

I was even an altar boy and choir boy at church, and I loved serving the Lord and praying to my Lord and His Mother, the Blessed Virgin.

Another great love was playing football, but I had a time of it for I was very small. It didn't matter, I played anyway. The local priest who was our coach showed us how to play. One of his main interests was to listen to classical music all the time when he wasn't busy doing his priestly things. Once in a while, he had to drive to Houston to his family-owned produce business. He always took a girl and a guy to ride with him, and I always enjoyed going with him on the ride. Lucky me, I got out of school for a while.

Still, another great love while growing up was water-skiing. My big sister and I use to go to a beautiful lake each summer in Louisiana to a quaint little town called New Roads. That place was heaven on earth. My aunt and uncle lived right near the lake with a pier to go fishing on. Needless to say, I went there every chance I could while I was growing up. I'll never forget the time I had fishing on that pier. Once, while fishing, I ran out of bait and I hadn't caught a thing. I started to quit, but I wondered if the fish would bite on a piece of bubble gum I was chewing. I put it on the hook and made my cast. Just as the gum splashed in the water, a huge large mouth bass hit it, and I was in for a ride landing him. Oh, what a thrill down the hill by the water's edge it was.

As time went by, I attended Kirwin High in Galveston. The Catholic high school was an all-boys school, and it was great for it was teamed up with not one, but two all-girls Catholic schools, Dominican and Ursuline High Schools. I knew where to go after our school let out. I had the best of both worlds, and I let it out with a shout, "YES." I thought girls were just great especially on a date for they knew how to kiss. I found out very early in life my vocation in life was not to be a priest.

After I graduated from high school, I went on to a co-ed college called Sam Houston State University in Huntsville, Texas. My biggest dream was fulfilled when I sat in my first class at the co-ed school and low and behold, the girls came in with a grin. I was not used to this, but I liked it a lot. My only problem was, I kept looking at the girls for they were like pearls, and my heart would do a lot of whirls. I went on from one girl to another until one day, I met the sweetheart pearl of them all. She had seen me on campus and asked a friend of mine if she could get her a date with me. I had already noticed her at the school hop, and I was about to pop. Of course, I would go out with her. Well, the date was set and I picked her up, and of all things, took her for a coke. Well, that little coke date was just great and it turned out to be a forty-year-long date. She was so fine as wine in the summertime. I was so blessed for she was the finest in the West, no less. It was love at first sight, and I loved her with all of my might. That's right, I flew higher than a kite. I had a convertible and on one special date, I took her to the lake where we ate, skate, and danced to the tunes of the Twist. At the time, that was my favorite chime, and I felt like I could shine if given the time. After the dance, I took her to see the submarines in the lake among the evergreens. Well, it was love at first sight, however, it began to rain cats and dogs, and I pushed the button to lift the car top but it would only drop; the battery was shot and I was a big flop—oh, what a sight in the night. We dated a lot and our grades went to pot. It didn't matter, I just needed to feel her touch so much whenever and forever. I just wanted her to be mine till the end of time.

One evening, we were embraced together, when she said, "Do we have any protection?"

My answer was "no," but I told her, "I want to marry you with or without a child inside for I want you to be my beautiful bride."

As things do, however, reality set in and she needed to go home to get a job in Houston as she was now pregnant and we knew not of abortion, but it didn't matter, we were going to get married without any commotion and the baby inside was sacred for the ride.

I drove to Houston to see her as much as I could for I wanted to be with my beautiful to-be bride, but her father and mother wanted me to take a long ride and not to ever be back by her side. You see, they wanted her to marry another young man from her high school. He was really a jock. I went to the store to buy her a ring that he could not top. I won out and she agreed to be my bride, and the church bells were ringing outside. We agreed to elope. One morning, I picked her up and we headed out, cutting the rope between her and her parents.

I drove to Galveston with her to see my mother and tell her our plan, but they weren't home. Like a dope I wrote her a note and left the isle with a smile. However, in Beaumont, Texas, I got cold feet because I didn't have a good plan, so I called her and told her our plan. She asked and we agreed to come home and get married correctly in the church and she would do the plan. It was a Catholic Church for I was a Catholic, however, my wife was a

Methodist, but she agreed to get married at our church. In order for us to get married, we had to go see a priest to make three promises, I believe. One was to raise our children as Catholics. My wife was not crazy about going to see the priest, but we went and discussed the issues at hand with him. He talked boastfully and read us our rights, so to speak. Things went pretty well for a while, but when he asked if we had any questions, my wife asked one which I don't even remember. All of a sudden, he stood up, quite angry, and turning red-faced he said, "All the churches were persecuting him and his church."

I didn't know what he was talking about and I didn't care. It wasn't a pretty sight. All I wanted to do was get the hell out of there. His impromptu actions made my wife hate the Catholic Church. All she really wanted to know was, could we kiss on the altar after we were married. He emphatically said no, we could not kiss until we got outside of the church. I knew the promises would never be kept and they weren't. She hated the Catholic Church for most of the rest of her life, and I was helpless and hopeless to persuading her otherwise. I really didn't try too hard for I knew the damage that priest did to us. All we wanted to do was just to get married peacefully. My plan to go to New Orleans wasn't such a bad plan, but we did get married in a Catholic Church in Galveston after all was said and done.

The wedding went off pretty well, but I had a hard time remembering my wife's name while trying to introduce her to our friends and family. I was a nervous wreck at twenty and couldn't even think of my own name.

The wedding pictures said it all because her dad looked like he had seen a ghost in church and was as depressed looking as one could be. Much later, he began to like me. I'll never forget his one question to me before my wife and I got married.

"Who do you put first, Jesus or your wife?" He did not like my answer for Jesus was always first in my life over everything, period, even my wife. Even today, I feel a husband and wife are together as one, but under Jesus, who is the one.

After we got married, we returned to college, and I thought we would live happily ever after. But little did I know for my wife left me after being together for only a week. She wanted to go home to see if she was still in love with her high school sweetheart who her parents wanted her to marry.

I would never forget that day she left to go back home for it snowed all day and there were hundreds of orange robins looking for something to eat in the snow. I watched the robins most of the day, crying my heart out for I loved my wife so much and I couldn't bear losing her. I decided to take action, so I drove to her home, opened the door, and demanded she come with me now or else... With much pressure she agreed to come back with me, and we made a go of it together for the next forty years. Well, things went pretty well for a short while until my wife came down with the German measles early on in her pregnancy. All she did was break out with a mild rash for a day or so. We didn't think too much of it at the time. However, a few months later, she started trying to have the baby prematurely on several occasions. Her doctor gave her an injection to hold off the delivery for as long as possible to give the baby a fighting chance to live after birth. She had a lot of false labor and one morning, I woke her and said, "I am going fishing but I will be back by noon. You'll be all right." That was an understatement of the year. While fishing, the Coast Guard boat approached our boat and they hollered, "Is there a Bill on board?" I said yes, and they hollered, "your wife is having a baby." Boy, was I ever in it for this fishing trip. I made it in plenty of time for she had an unusual long delivery. When our sweet little baby was born, the nurse brought him to the viewing window and all cheered with delight. Oh, what a beautiful sight. I was on cloud nine until our baby's doctor came on board and said, "We have a problem. It seems that the Ruebella or German measles caused the baby's internal organs to all be in the wrong places and we need to call in a specialist because his heart is where his stomach should be." She got a hold of Dr. Denton Cooly, and he checked the baby out and said, "We will operate tomorrow if he lives through the night." Well, he didn't and he passed about 10:00 P.M. to be with Jesus. I couldn't take it too well and something inside me said to go see little Bill, so about 2:00 A.M., I went to the nurse's station and asked to see my baby boy. They got him and I asked to hold him, and they let me. I lifted my baby high as I could and I told the Lord, "Here is my firstborn boy, I give him to you. Please, Lord, I don't know what else to do." My next step was to comfort my wife as best as I could. The hardest part I think was having to pick out a baby coffin for him to lay in. We had to have a full-blown funeral just as an adult would have. It was hard and all I really remembered was bending over and kissing little William goodbye and thinking how precious life really is. We should never take it for granted. A couple of years later, my wife wanted to try again to have a baby even though she had big doubts about her being able to have a healthy baby, but she did and we had a beautiful little daughter. She was a grand welcome to come into our life, especially after losing our little boy. She did just fine until she was two, and she started having very high fever, 106 °F and above. The doctor checked her out and said she needed to see a specialist right away for she was having urinary tract problems. She got a hold of Dr. Herbert Seybold and he said, "We need to operate right away. It seems her bladder valves are not working and an immediate surgery is eminent for her to get over the fever." The tests that were given her were horrible for her. She endured much pain both before and after the nine-hour surgery. Thank God, the surgery went well and new valves were made from her bladder lining. I have never witnessed such pain and suffering like she had. For three days, she was bowed up in bed with her head and feet only touching the bed. The doctor was merciful and he removed the tubes in her two days early for he hadn't seen such suffering either. He was the best doctor my daughter could have had; he lived in my hometown in Galveston. So far, she has never had any more urinary tract infections and seems to be doing just fine, and I am proud of her because I know she is in good standing with her Lord and Savior.

My other daughter was born four years after my first daughter, and my wife had a good pregnancy and all was thought to be going well but later, our daughter did poorly in school. When she was in the second grade, we had some tests run on her to see what her problem was. All I got out of it was she did not hear all of the words when she was spoken to and she could not follow directions. She had it very hard until she quit school in the eleventh grade. Years later, however, she got her GED and went on to college part-time and of all things on various scholarships. She has now earned her associates degree in psychology and is on board to finishing her bs degree. What an evolution this has been for her and I am very proud of her especially for her determination to get through school on her own.

Now then, when my children were still young, my wife and I both decided they should be raised Methodists and go to church with my wife. I had to give in for the priest's actions left negative impressions on both of us. My wife and children went to the Methodist Church each Sunday while I went alone to my Catholic Church. I kept going each Sunday alone and I felt awful inside for all I could see was other children with their parents in church being happily together as a family.

I think this was when I turned my back on the Catholic Church as I left one Sunday in the middle of the mass not to return for twenty-five years or so later, I left the church but I always looked for God for help. I didn't totally abandon him.

My wife and I continued to have much suffering for she got very sick with Chronic Fatigue Syndrome and she was convalescing a good part of her life even a lot on her back in bed. For a while, she even had to have catheters for her to be able to urinate. She was so sick; I had to put the catheters in for her. This was difficult for she couldn't even walk. I had to hold her up to keep her from falling. I loved her so much especially when she took care of me when I was so sick.

Now it's my turn, I suppose. I was in a car mishap and my car crushed my ankle and scraped off most of my ankle bone. I was sent to the hospital and underwent surgery at midnight. The surgery went pretty well, but the pain after recovery was out of sight and out of mind. I was hurt so bad, I couldn't walk and I needed a lot of morphine to get me through the day. I went home after five days in the hospital but without the morphine to help me. They gave me a pain killer, but it did little to take away the pain. I asked the doctor how long it would take to get addicted to the pain medicine. He asked how many days was it from the accident. I told him twenty-seven days and he said I needed to stop on the twenty-seventh day. I went to physical therapy for a month, but they didn't help at all but only dished out much pain and suffering. They said that was all they could do for me, which was nothing.

I couldn't walk without crutches, so I went to a neighborhood hotel and asked them if I could come each day and walk in the water. They said it was all right with them, so I went walking in the swimming pool up to my neck. I gradually got better over six weeks of pain and graduated to shallower water, a little at a time, and then to the baby pool where I was walking normally again. I am not sure whether the water-walking or God was to get credit for I was walking again. Probably both, for it was a miracle.

My wife and I quit drinking in August 1988 and we went to AA. I also attended the Alanon program with its twelve steps. I attended many meetings in both programs and was helped a lot especially in the fourth step—one of confession of lifelong sins and ending resentments in one's life. I came to the conclusion that all the bad things I did in my life, I did it while drinking, so if I wanted to live right, I had to stop getting tight. I was severely handicapped in these meetings because I was practically deaf and I couldn't relate to what others were saying. I was also very scared to talk. I decided I needed another program where I didn't have to hear and speak and I found it in Jesus' program where he was in command and He held out his hand when we walked together on the sand at the beach. His awesome might became my greatest delight. I now have twenty one years of sobriety and I thank God, my Almighty.

It was mid-August 1988, when my wife and I finally went on a real honeymoon vacation in Cancun, Mexico. The water there was as beautiful as it can be. God worked overtime to make it so majestic. When I woke up and saw it, I climbed out on the ledge of the window of the hotel and just stared at it. I couldn't believe my eyes were seeing this much beauty. The water even seemed to glow in places where it was shallow and you could even see the fish in the water. I'll never forget it as long as I live. Hopefully, before I die I'll make another visit to that little bit of heaven on earth. Oh what a sight that was.

By this time, we had been married twenty-five years and had two children, a dog, and a cat. I thought we had the perfect marriage; but then, one day, my wife blurted out, "I love you, but I'm not in love with you."

Needless to say, I was heartbroken upon hearing such news and I didn't rightly know what to say or do. Shortly thereafter, I went to my desk to make a phone call when I looked down on the nearby table and there was a spiral notebook just sitting there. I was curious about it, so I picked it up and opened it in the middle, where I saw her handwriting in it. I couldn't believe my eyes when I read it and it said, "I am going to meet with my high school sweetheart at the upcoming twenty-fifth high school reunion. I couldn't believe what I was reading for I thought my marriage was a pretty good one. You never know, I guess. Perhaps, the ultimatum I gave her long ago kept her from finding out whether she loved him or not. I confronted her about the notebook and she admitted her feelings to me and said she was going to meet with him at the reunion.

The school reunion came pretty quickly and we sat at our table near where he and his wife and two children were seated. I thought how disgusting it was for him to try and get together with my wife right near where his family was seated. I then heard an announcement over the PA system for all graduates to come to another room nearby where they would be taking group pictures. My wife excused herself and walked to the photo room and crossed paths with him and they started talking to each other. I couldn't watch and I wanted to give her the space she needed to do her thing, so I went outside for a smoke and sat on a bench for about an hour. I cried real hard over this. I then went back and asked her if she knew anything now. She said she didn't know but they would be getting together in two weeks for dinner when he would be back in town on business.

A couple days later, on Labor Day, Monday, I woke up early and had coffee. I then decided this was too much for me to deal with in two more weeks, so I wrote her a note about this and left in my car to go for a drive to cool off a bit. I drove calmly to the corner and turned left when I gunned my car a little. I then made another corner when I really gunned it for I was losing it, I think. My hands started trembling a lot. I thought I had better pull off the road fast so as not to lose it and get into a car wreck. I pulled into a parking lot in front of a building with concrete sides. As I stopped in front of the wall, I began to see images on the wall. About twelve empty squares appeared outlined in red and I immediately thought this was a form of hell appearing on the wall. I then thought I must belong in one of the squares for I had turned my back on the church long ago and I thought I didn't need it. Just then a sharp pain began to go across my chest where my heart is. I really got scared then I began to cry out "I want you, I need you, I need you now, speaking to Jesus." The cry was mine but I didn't know where the words came from. I didn't think them, I just said them. When I said the word "now" a bright white light encompassed me in and around my car, and it flowed into the top of my head through my body and back out of my head. As the amazing light went through me, all of the trembling and chest pains left me immediately. With my eyes closed, I began to see a vision of a green concave line with two dots on the top, which I immediately said those must be my two children. Further down the line was a little larger dot, which I named my wife and below that was a dot for me. After a second, there appeared to the right of my wife another dot, her high school sweetheart with a line connecting both of them. I watched for a while then I said, "Go" and the dot and line between them disappeared for a couple of seconds but then came back. I re-emphasized once again, "Go now" and it did but came back again. This time, I was more emphatic and I said, "Go now forever," and it did and never came back. I then saw a vision of two red hearts side by side and then shooting toward heaven. I then saw a vision of a descending Paraclete from heaven or a form like a dove or the Holy Spirit coming down vertically from above. The visions ended and I could sense it was dark again outside.

   I opened my eyes and looked out of my side window. I could tell the sun had just came up and was being blocked by the thick trees nearby. Apparently, the sun could have been the bright white light, but I don't think so. I could feel it going through my body like a flowing liquid. I didn't know what to think so I drove my car back home in wonderment of what had taken place that morning in my car. I felt I must have suffered a nervous breakdown with an unexplained spontaneous healing. I drove home and told my wife what had happened to me that day and she thought I was a little crazy. I didn't blame her for thinking that, perhaps, maybe I was. But then, I held onto the visions in my heart and came to believe it was a Spiritual Event from above.

Meanwhile, two weeks went by and she met with her ex and they had lunch together. She came home with the good news that she loved me not him and this would be the end of that, just like the vision predicted. This was good news to me, and our marriage lasted another fifteen years in spite of all the strange things that happened to us, until she passed away on Memorial Day in 2004.

Chapter Two

Major Depression

My wife didn't believe the Spiritual Event scenario and suggested I should see a doctor immediately, which I did, and he put me on a drug to relieve my high anxiety that I started having. As I took more of it, the more anxious I got, and on and on. The drug quit working and I was totally addicted to it, so I tried getting off the drug. It took me a month mostly in bed to wean down to just half pill a day and I had gotten very depressed from all of this.

    I was then hospitalized with a major depression and was put on several prescriptions to fight the depression and calm the high anxiety I had. I left the hospital after three weeks and went home to recover. The depression was so bad, I could not function very well and I couldn't return to work. The days turned into weeks and weeks into months and I wasn't getting any better. I felt so bad, I wanted to die and I would walk around my neighborhood block and hope a car going by on a busy street would jump the curb and do me in. But then, I thought I probably wouldn't get killed, but it would only make me worse off for I thought I had the worse luck possible and I wouldn't die from it. Every thought I had was a negative one with no positive thoughts. I kept saying "I think I can, I think I can," like the little red engine that could but I knew I couldn't. I walked around all day carrying a heavy load of depression on my back. Everything looked black, gray, and dismal. I couldn't smile. I looked thirty years older than I used too and I had given up on ever getting well again. It seemed like the more I tried, the worse I became and the more I wanted to die. Adjusting and or changing the medications didn't help. All I could do was cry and cry, "Why couldn't I just die." Soon thereafter, I got scared of dying and not going to heaven, but perhaps, even to that fiery place, no one would want to go too. Well, I surely didn't want to go there.

After having not gone to church in twenty-five years, I decided to give it a try, what could I lose? I walked to my first mass about a mile and went inside with the rest of the church-going people. It was no big deal, but I felt my depression slack off a bit during the Communion time of the Mass. I didn't go to communion but I still felt better, and feeling better was a luxury indeed, to me. I walked back home and by the time I came to my block, my depression was just as bad as before I went to church. This was depressing in itself, but I learned that Mass helped me.

Now, I wanted to go to communion, so I went to confession with a very nice priest. Confessing my sins for the last twenty-five years wasn't so easy, but I tried and when I finished confession, I felt no better than before. I just didn't feel forgiven and that was all important to me. I knew in my heart, if I could feel forgiven, my depression would get better. Well, the first confession did nothing for my depression, so I was determined to try again at a later date.

Meanwhile, I started to hang out in St. Cecilia's Catholic Church after the congregation would leave. I went to the first row just under a huge cross with Jesus on it and I cried to him "Why oh why did this happen to me?" Of course, there was no answer for me, but I cried anyway because I felt so sad inside and once again, I wanted to feel glad inside. I said my rosary often at church and even when I walked along the neighborhood blocks. I noticed when I prayed I just felt better. The depression would not leave me for when I stopped praying, it came back and I often had panic attacks.

Since when I went to confession, I started receiving communion at every Mass often two or three times in one day. I kept doing this over and over because when I did receive communion, I felt better if only for a short while. A little meant a lot to me, for nothing else would make me feel well. Again, I went to church by myself, even at night. They stayed open till 10:00 P.M. and I closed it nearly every night. I kept crying for God to help me with my depression. The walls in the church would often bang and creek, scaring me half to death, but I wouldn't leave because I felt safe with Jesus up there on the cross in church. This went on for months until one day, instead of crying "Why me, Lord?" I cried, why you, Lord? After all, you were God and you didn't have to suffer and die for me. Out of love you chose this misery for my sins, no less. You didn't deserve to suffer so much but I'll bet your mental suffering was just as severe as your physical suffering, perhaps, worse for you must have suffered a major depression just thinking that you would be dying for those who hate you, or those who didn't even want to know you."

    I didn't spend all my time in church because I once went to a health club to try and exercise, hoping against hope that it would help me. I went inside of the dressing room and changed clothes. I went over to the stationary bicycle to exercise. After five minutes, I got exhausted and called it quits. I sat down inside the dressing room to change back to my street clothes when I noticed an old man in the mirror and I felt sorry for him until I realized the old looking man was me. I raced home to tell my wife but she started laughing and laughing and got me to start laughing as well. This laugh was a blessing to me for it was the first sign I had that I might be getting better because I couldn't laugh at all before. I had hope once again that the end of my depression might be near.

    With all that was going on with me, it was putting a real strain on my wife for she had to listen to it all and it scared her, too. None of us knew what to do. She decided to get away from it all, so she took a trip to New Roads where she would be with my mother and sister. This frightened me because I hadn't been alone before in this illness. On the first night I was alone, I decided to go to the ball fields to watch some fast-pitch girls softball games. I had been a coach and umpire at these fields for over ten years, but I had quit when my daughters stopped playing. As

I drove up to the fields, I saw an old umpire friend of mine umpiring a game. During the inning switch, he called me over and asked me how I was doing. I told him "Not so good" because I was suffering from a major depression. He was surprised and he told me he went through the same thing a few years ago. He suggested I start umpiring immediately for it would be good for my depression. I told him I would like to give it a try, so he lined me up with a ball game the next week. Meanwhile, my wife got home and I told her I was going to ump again. She thought this was a good idea and we went to the first ball game together. As we were standing behind the dugout, I got scared I couldn't do it. I started to panic, but my wife got me settled down. My legs were getting very heavy like lead weights. The time came and I entered the infield. hardly being able to walk. As I squatted down behind home plate, I was a bag of shattered nerves. I really didn't want to be here. It was now time, so I yelled out "Play ball!" As the first pitch came zooming in, I yelled "Steeee rike" and my nervousness and heavy legs vanished because I had loved umpiring so much and my mind was on the game instead of on poor old me. This was a positive influence and I now knew I was going to get better.

With this new ray of hope, I felt a good confession would be the ticket, so I went back to church and confessed my sins again. I just happened to go to the same nice priest as before and when he heard these sins again, he knew it was me. He heard me out and then he stood up and told the Lord to remove these sins from my back and put them on his back. With that, I felt at last, forgiven and I left the church a happier person, but I still had a little doubt until the next day when I returned to the cross to pray to my Lord and Savior. I went to the first pew and before I could kneel, I looked up and saw a huge curtain of red stringed blood droplets coming down from the ceiling, in between the cross and me, all the way across the width of the church. I couldn't imagine what was happening, so I looked down to see if the curtain went all the way to the floor. It didn't because it stopped halfway down. When I looked back up to see the curtain, it was gone and it could not be seen. The only sight was a circular light around the statue of Jesus' heart up on the cross, which I felt was an expression of his love for me. I didn't know how to feel, so I humbly returned to my car and that's when I found out evil was about to shout because I saw on the pavement below me was the face of Satan. Little did I know what was now in store for me, but it came swiftly to me. The first signs after that were writings on the walls of the concrete storm sewers, basically warning me evil was coming from below and it would be quite a show.

But first on the day after the curtain of blood droplets appeared and disappeared, which reminded me that all of my sins were forgiven and forgotten, I was leaving the church with my rosary in hand when a young lady came up to me and asked have you been to Medjugorie. I said, "No, where's that?" She said, my rosary had turned gold like they were doing in Medjugorie where the Blessed Virgin was appearing to several seers. I was impressed no less and when I went to another church that evening, I asked the priest what did the gold mean. He said, "Gold is for forgiveness or refining and I took that to mean for the last time my sins <u>have</u> <u>truly</u> <u>been</u> <u>forgiven</u>." I am a hard case but it took all of this to convince me of God's Divine Mercy for me and his Divine Love for me. I now feel it in my heart and I don't doubt anymore. After all, he is God and if he wants to forgive me, who am I to say he can't or won't. He will and does forgive all who humbly ask him for forgiveness and he does this out of his love for us. He loves us all for that is why he made us to know love and serve him, and he wants us to be with him—one day—in his heavenly home he made for us.

Now then, while I was at this church, I was told by two ladies there to go to the Catholic Charismatic Center across town. I later went to the Charismatic Center and attended church services and was so impressed, I asked my wife to go with me. After much convincing, she agreed to go. The next week, as we were getting ready to leave for church and as she was getting into the car she said she really didn't want to go. I looked up at the heavens and said, "Lord this is your last chance for you to get her to go." With that, she said she would go just once and she did.

While we were standing in our pew during the service, the priest came up to her and said a prayer. My wife fell over backward along with four pews of other people around her who fell back behind her. Several churchgoers as well as, my wife, cried tears of joy for the Holy Spirit had slain them and brought them into the fold of Jesus. After this, she was always ready to go to the Center and we became regulars. I believe the name of the priest was Father McDonnah and I thanked him for his prayers and baptism of my wife in the Holy Spirit. My wife's spiritual life was changed forever and it even helped her deal with what was happening to me every day through my walk with the Lord and the awesome distractions of evil ones that followed me wherever I would go, day and night.

Chapter Three

Good and Evil

The next morning, I woke up from a deep sleep and above me in the room was a cross with Jesus on it rotating in a circular motion in the air, and it was all lit up with lights and the cross would turn to and from and change colors. Usually, the cross was lit up red or purple and I began to pray very hard the Hail Marys and when I prayed, the colors would sometimes turn white as snow as if sins were being forgiven, or these were souls in Purgatory being freed as a result of our prayers. I don't rightly know what it meant but it was beautiful yet, sad for my Lord was still on the cross, no less. Surely, I thought he could not still be suffering on his cross for us.

After a while of praying and looking at the beautiful cross inside, I got up and went outside on my patio. When I looked up to the heavens, there was the cross again, high in the sky with Jesus on it and I began to pray again, not knowing what was happening to me for seeing such a sight.

I prayed real hard until I wore out and looked down to the ground, and there, before me, everything around had turned for the worse. The patio was all cracked up, the house needed painting, most of the trees had died, and all the grass was burned up. I went into my house and everything was out of place. The pictures on the wall were all crooked, clothes were thrown throughout the house, walls needed painting, and the furniture was out of its usual place. Amazingly, my wife saw all of these happenings as being normal to her.

I went out of my house to see what I could see around the neighborhood. It was awful all over because the sidewalks were all crooked and cracked, a lot of the trees had died, all the grass was dead and there was the smell of oil in the air. Most of the houses needed painting and repairs and nearly everything had changed for the worse. Most of the automobiles were dented, and in need of paint.

I didn't know it at the time, but the world around me had changed for the worse and almost everything looked evil and vile.

I soon found out the only things that looked normal to me were the sun, the moon, and the sea along with of all things the American and Texas flags, which were and still are always beautiful to me. The word Texas was special to me and sometimes when I saw it, the word "Texas," I would be filled with joy.

The anxiety caused by all of these events was overwhelming, and I was scared to death by the enormity of it all and the evil of it all. One evening, my wife wanted to go out for dinner, so we drove up to a Mexican restaurant nearby. The name on the restaurant was missing some letters and I knew I was in for a time in there. We went in and the floors and tables were uneven and everything was wrong inside. We ordered our food and I got what I always liked: tacos, beans, and rice. When we got served, I started eating my food when suddenly, some of it turned bitter as if vinegar had been poured on some, but not all of my food. It was awful. My wife asked why wasn't I eating my food and I was afraid to tell her because her food was normal to her and all around her was normal to her. It soon became obvious to me that I was the only one who saw all of this destruction and devastation. I could not let on to her what I was seeing because she would think I was crazy, so I kept my mouth shut and ate my bitter food then we went home. She saw nothing of the evil around us and could care less about the trees and grass dying before my eyes. Seeing all of these things out of place was not okay to me but was okay with her. I believe, she thought I was losing it and I wondered it, too.

After we got home, I told my wife I wanted to walk to the nearby store to buy a pack of cigarettes. This was only an excuse to get out of the house and observe any new developments in the night that might take place. Sure enough, on my way back from the store, there was a bright star in the sky hovering above me but not very high as the other stars were. I ran home with my nerves shattered to bits. I tried to watch television but it was impossible because I would turn on a channel and all evil prevailed on it. I then changed channels to something good but the good channels turned to evil channels too. It was too mind-boggling to watch as I had become to hate evil and I could not watch it, not even for a second. I got up and went outside in disgust.

I also had trouble with advertisement signs along the highway as some good signs would be uplifting, but then, there were those that were evil, which were depressing. I tried not to look at the signs as best as I could because it boggled my mind.

I had read about ecstasies and I think I experienced them often because when I saw something especially Godly, I would swell up inside and wanted to cry with joy. This happened to me upon seeing the word "Star," which sometimes happened just when I needed to see it. The same occurred when I saw the word "Crown," as if I might be a star and might wear a crown one day, if I followed Jesus all the way. These overwhelming feelings sometimes happened in church when I would feel God's love while watching a picture of Jesus called, "The Risen Christ." Whenever I experienced an ecstasy, I would thank Jesus just like Gomer Pyle did, saying over and over, "Thank you, thank you, thank you!" There was a special song when I heard it, it filled me with peace and joy and it was called "Work of Heart." It was about God who was the artist and I was his canvass; he drew a work of heart on me and painted love and sunshine around me and wiped away all my sins.

From the start and even today, I often hear choirs of angels singing and playing beautiful music in my ears, but sometimes, the evil takes over and sings the same tune over and over again, trying to drive me crazy. I have gotten use to their tactics, and prayers usually drive these evil sounds out of my ears, making me okay.

With all of this going on, my wife and I decided I should see another psychiatrist and his name was Dr. S., a children's psychiatrist of Jewish descent. He was just right for me because he prescribed the same medicine I am taking even today, twenty-one years later. Above all, though he would listen to me hours on end about my adventure in the never-world, he never once challenged me on what I saw and felt around me, even though he must have thought of me a bit off. I knew all along these things were really happening to me even though it was unbelievable at first. Without him being put into my life, I don't know what I would have done. He heard it all and strengthened me in my plight with evil all around me, and the Jesus part of it didn't seem to bother him a bit even though he was a Jew. I was so very thankful he came into my life when he did. But today, I am saddened because he moved away to further his practice and I have lost all contact with him. May God bless him dearly. Before he left, he introduced me to Dr. T who has been prescribing my medications and checking me out ever since. He is a very fine doctor also and I wouldn't have made it without both of them. I take my medications as prescribed because I don't want to ever get another major depression again. I wouldn't wish that on my worst enemy.

Now, getting back to the evil distractions, at first, the evil people scared me to death because I had not known such evil existed. They would follow me wherever I would go, trying to scare me and distract me from my walk with my Lord and they were very successful at first. They would cross my path wherever I walked and even wherever I drove. The anxiety caused by them nearly did me in. I couldn't watch them, so I tried my best to ignore them whenever they showed up. It was at this time I walked the streets praying inwardly to Jesus and the evil ones followed me. Each day, whenever I would close my eyes to rest them, evil faces of never before seen evil creatures would appear in front of me and I would be face to face with the hideous faces and the skin on their evil faces would be peeled off their faces like melting wax, leaving only their skulls and bones showing. Every night before I went to sleep, these faces would appear for a while, and the evil visions would then leave until morning, so I could go to sleep at night. If the faces hadn't disappeared, I would never have gone to sleep. This was an awful sight to see and it frightened me a lot. Often times, when I closed my eyes to go to sleep or have them closed while waking up, I would see evil people doing various things. When I would look at them to see what they were, the evil would smile and walk toward me, do all kinds of hideous things to warp my mind and scare me. If I wanted to go to sleep, the only way to avoid this situation was to open my eyes. I couldn't keep opening my eyes or I would never have gone to sleep. I solved this by glancing away from the evil with my eyes shut. After a fashion I got used to it, so to speak and I would go to sleep while looking at the evil anyway face to face and eye to eye and only then would it dissapear.

When I would go outside, the evil often drove in their dented and tattered cars passing by me over and over and with all of this confusion, I would get scared and seek refuge in my house. One time I went to the Home Depot on a weekend and I was in the store admiring the overhead light fixtures when all of a sudden I found myself being converged on by the evil ones. I ran out of the store and went home as fast as I could. Being hemmed in caused me much anxiety and I couldn't handle it very well, so I never went into big stores on weekends again.

The medications didn't help my anxiety, so I started to face it head on, but I now had a secret weapon to help me through even the worst of it and that was my Hail Marys. Whenever I would see evil, I started to pray nonstop over and over, until the evil subsided and it usually did after a fashion. In addition to this, I started looking up at the sun and moon high above because there was no evil in them. They stood high in the sky and never changed from good to evil like the world around me did. At first, I was torn apart for looking up at the sun and moon while praying; seemed to be like praying to an idol. I walked and prayed, always trying not to look at the sun, but I couldn't. The evil around me was too intense and I had to ignore it the best I could, or I would have been scared to death. I told God over and over again, I was not praying to the sun and moon, for they were no more than a representation of my God Almighty and Jesus Christ, respectively. When I prayed outside I always looked up at the sun for it never changed to evil. The sun was eye-soothing instead of eye-burning. It seemed to have a mirror like reflection that stopped the burning rays from blinding me, so I walked and walked, looking up, so I wouldn't see the evil around me trying to hem me in and do me in. Another trial about the sun was I was told from youth not to look at the sun because it would cause me to go blind. I didn't want to lose my sight but I didn't want to look at the evil either because it would have made me crazy. I guess being blind would be better than being scared to death, so I looked at the sun anyway. Thank God I didn't go blind. I then began looking at the moon which was a representation of my Lord, Jesus Christ while praying my Hail Marys. The moon reminded me of the white Host or Holy Communion, and the love of Jesus for me. In any case, at night, I felt Jesus was with me and showing me from above that he loved me very much. I was no longer scared in the night from fright because I was in His light and he would protect me from the evil sight around me.

The sea around me reminded me of the Holy Spirit since we were baptized with water, and it was so peaceful to me. I feared no other when I was near the sea looking and praying upward toward the sun and moon which were so beautiful to me. Whenever I was alone on the beach by the sea, the evil kept its distance from me, seemingly knowing I was in contact with my Lord and Savior and they didn't want any part of that. Often times I would go to the beach to get closer to my Lord. I would park my car, watch the sunrise and pray or listen to music on my car radio. It was amazing that the best music would fill my ear as the sun first came out in the morning to light the world.

After a couple of hours of praying and listening to my music, I would call it quits and start to leave. It was at this time God would often express himself by showing me flocks of ducks, pelicans, and doves. I would always leave feeling better and I knew God was there and was always watching over me. Once as I was about to leave the beach at sunrise, I started backing my car to leave. It was then I saw the most beautiful rainbow I have ever seen and it was touching the ground no more than thirty feet from my car. I found out there was no pot of gold at the end of the rainbow, just me. As I drove home, I often looked at the sun while driving, so I wouldn't get bothered by many traffic jams that often occurred. No traffic jam on the way could cause me to blow my top. Praying made the trip go by just wonderful, no matter what I came in contact with. The evil could not get to me no matter how hard it tried and I was glad of that because I had a weapon that worked for me, my prayers.

On one occasion, believe it or not, I got into my automobile to drive away from the church when I looked and saw the pavement in front of my car start to split apart and come my way like a mini earthquake. All of a sudden, before the split pavement reached my car, my car lifted up in the air with me in it for just a few seconds while the split in the pavement went under me. I was then let gently down to the ground and drove away in wonderment of all of God's power and lack of power the evil actually had over me. It left me no doubt God could do anything he wanted to do. He had no limitations but the evil did because they, too, were under his control for boundaries were apparently set by God, so they couldn't harm me.

On another occasion, I was riding on the ferry for pleasure when I saw a large captain inside a boat drawing close to me near the ferry. He was driving his boat diagonally across and at the rear of the ferry, very fast. The name of his boat was TEXAS. I was overwhelmed with ecstasy for Texas was so special to me and I associated it with Jesus; after all, he was a Lone Star too, just like how we were so proud of our Lone Star State, I was proud of my Lord, too. The captain was bigger than life and he reminded me of Matt Dillon of Gunsmoke who was dauntless and unafraid while controlling the good and evil in his territory. He was the good and in-charge of the bad and he was in total control over both.

Early on in this fiasco, when I would go to my church, the church bells would often start to ring and ring and ring, just as I grabbed the church's door handle. This was awesome to behold and I sometimes had an ecstasy during this as the bells would not stop ringing for a long time and I didn't know why this was happening to me.

One day, I went to church to pray in the adoration room. While I was in there, I picked up a pamphlet that spoke of the Divine Mercy of Jesus, which I read and it was so beautiful to me. Apparently, a nun named Sister Faustina received in a vision, Jesus' favorite prayers about his Divine Mercy for us. He told her to say his prayers everyday at 3:00 P.M., the time the Lord died on the cross, and that person praying would receive forgiveness for his sins. God's very words to her were "My heart overflows with great mercy for souls, and especially for poor sinners…It is for them that my blood and water flowed from my heart as from a fount overflowing with mercy. The Feast of Mercy emerged from my very depths of tenderness. It is my desire that it be solemnly celebrated on the first Sunday after Easter." Part of the prayer goes like this:

"For the sake of his sorrowful passion, have mercy on us, and on the whole world."

I then began to say this prayer in addition to the million Hail Marys I must have said throughout this ordeal. The new prayer given to us by Jesus himself was a welcomed new prayer and I started saying it at least a million times. Prayer was my life throughout all of this. Without prayer, I would have sunk in the mire of the depths of the evils' desire and my soul may have been lost.

The evil had their large Dobermans ready to attack me, and God alone stopped the dogs from harming me. Once, however, one such dog broke away and ran directly to me, growling as he charged. He got to me and attacked my hand and bit it furiously. However, there was no pain and when he retreated, my hand was left intact as if I had never been bitten. There was no blood, no teeth marks, nothing. I was okay, as if nothing had happened. Needless to say I had a prayer of thankfulness to my Lord for saving me and I grew less afraid of the evil, now that I knew God was out to protect me. I was not alone and I now knew it.

On Good Friday in 1989, I drove to Galveston, Texas and went to church. I went inside to pray while a wedding was in process on the day Christ died. Weddings are not allowed on Good Friday. As I entered the church, I could feel the evil there inside the church. I left as soon as I could and went to the beach to pray.

I decided to get out of my car on the beach with my dog and I started to walk and pray the Divine Mercy and the Hail Marys. I walked about a mile or two and came upon the ocean's sea in front of me. I wondered for a moment if I could walk on water like St. Peter did, so I tried real hard not to doubt and I took a step in the water and my foot sank immediately just as it should. I smiled and thought, *oh, well, what the hell, I had to try anyway*. I decided to walk in the water looking up to the sun but it was behind some clouds. I kept praying anyway and the clouds opened up and I could see the sun directly above me. I grew tired of praying, so I stopped and the clouds closed up blocking the sun once again. I started praying again as the clouds opened up again exposing the sun and the sun moved closer, just above me. When I tried again, the same thing happened. I finally quit praying and I turned to see if the evil was near me. It wasn't for it was as if the evil knew when I needed to be alone with my God. On another occasion, I was watching the sunset and the sun was just about to set behind the curvature of the earth when I started to pray very hard. Upon doing this, the sun stopped setting and just stood there until I stopped praying, and it then set immediately. I read in the bible where this happened to Joshua I believe, but the sun stopped setting all day while he fought a battle. It's in the bible.

Speaking of the bible, I had never read the bible before, for Catholics usually heard the bible in church at Mass. Since I hadn't gone to mass in twenty-five years, I knew nothing of the bible but something inside me propelled me to get a bible to read. The only bible I had was one with too many "these and thou's" and it was too hard to understand, so I went to a nearby bible store and looked through many of the bibles. I came across one that interested me for it was written in common English and it was called the New International Version or NIV Bible Student Version. Since I was a student at this point, I bought it and immediately began reading it. I started from the beginning in Genesis and read through Exodus and then the Psalms and Proverbs along with Isaiah, Ezekiel, Daniel, Jeremiah, and all the New Testament highlighting all that were important to me. I was amazed at how God's love projected itself throughout the bible. Surely, there were dark days in the bible and the Lord God seemed to be very steadfast at times but his actions were his and he is God and God can do whatever God wants because he is God and he is like no other. What he did was out of love for us and that was why he gave us Jesus, his only Son to redeem us from our sins. Anyway, I read the bible each night before retiring and reading it often tired me to sleep. I knew I couldn't learn the bible in total, so I didn't try. Instead, I let the Holy Spirit take me to where he wanted me to go in the bible. I highlighted all that meant the most to me and have only reread the highlighted portions, saving me a lot of time to cover what I need to cover. I can hardly ever remember the chapter and verse, but I usually remember where the verse is located in the bible. Sometimes, I feel the Holy Spirit has taught me just what I need to know and no more for that is enough in itself. I do feel that Jesus didn't just die on the cross to be dead in heaven. I do believe both Jesus and his Blessed Mother have appeared on earth to special people to carry on his word for us. I can't believe God shut up forever at the end of the bible. He even said in the bible if all was written about him, it would take the whole world to hold all the books written about him. I feel the bible was not and is not the only word of God but it is the main book we have about him, and his words are magnificent, for he is our God Almighty and he gave us his Word in the bible for us to know how he loves and forgives us through his Son, Jesus. There is no other like him and there will be no other like him after all he made us, he looks out for us and he promises his heaven for us who stand by him to the end. Amen.

    Now, getting back to the good, early on, I started seeing two wheels in my eyes and also in the sky whenever I looked high above and whenever I closed my eyes, the wheels spin around and around on its axis and intersect while spinning and sometimes they have beautiful colors. When the wheels in the sky turned over, a cool breeze would blow in my face like the breath of God was around me. I have come to believe these wheels are symbols of the Holy Spirit and the Glory of God. The wheels sometimes turn into wings—like that of a beautiful dove—in my eyes when closed and whenever I looked high in the sky, birds of all kinds flew between and into and around the wheels, making a delightful sight. Whenever I looked up in the sky at the clouds rolling by, the clouds would turn into faces of creatures like images that I surely have never seen before or perhaps, by anyone else. As the wheels faced the creatures, it would turn the faces against each other and they would move to and from until the image disappeared in the wind. I didn't understand this then or even now, but I think it was like what the prophet Ezekiel saw when he experienced the power of God in the desert. He said, "As I looked at the living creatures, I saw a wheel on the ground beside each creature with its four faces. This was the appearance and structure of the wheels: They sparkled like chrysolite and all four looked alike. Each appeared to be made like a wheel intersecting a wheel. As they moved, they would go in any one of four directions the creatures faced; the wheels did not turn about as the creatures went. There rims were high and awesome, and all four rims were full of eyes all around. When the living creatures moved, the wheels beside them moved; and when the living creatures rose from the ground, the wheels also rose. Wherever the spirit would go, they would go, and the wheels would rise along with them, because the spirit of the living creatures was in the wheels....When the creatures moved, I heard the sound of their wings, like the roar of rushing waters, like the voice of the Almighty...and this was like the appearance of the glory of the Lord....Then the cherubim, with the wheels beside them, spread their wings and the Glory of the God of Israel was above them." I didn't experience the exact same vision Ezekiel experienced, but it was close enough to realize I was seeing the Glory of the Lord. Unlike me, God spoke to Ezekiel telling him exactly what he wanted him to do in the light of Israel's turning its back on God. In my case, he had only spoken to me once, not in a bolt of lightning and loud thunder but in a sweet gentle voice saying to me as if coming from a radio left turned on, and the voice of God said softly, "One day at a time." When hearing this, I knew it was the Lord's voice. I had no doubt and the radio wasn't even turned on. I felt a sigh of relief that he would walk and talk with me throughout my journey with the never-land and hopefully beyond in his heavenly home.

On two occasions, over the period of two or three hours, a huge cloud in the sky would form into the shape of a dragon which I have come to believe was a representation of Satan himself. Why this was shown to me, I have no idea, but it was. The dragon is mentioned once in Revelations, "Then another sign appeared in heaven, an enormous red dragon with seven heads and ten horns and seven crowns appeared." I have no idea what the appearance of two dragons would mean but I saw them nevertheless.

Along with the beautiful wheels, I have come to believe that God communicates with me through his wondrous works of nature like in doves, ducks, or pelicans or even in rainbows. He often uplifts my heart when one is shown to me, usually out of the clear blue and when it's most unexpected. He likes to deliver these signs to me when I am on my last leg and need assurance the most from him to go on. He never fails me, but he likes to deliver at the final moment when he assures me he is still with me and we have more to do. Once, while I was at the beach, flocks of doves would fly just over my head and this was very uplifting because to me, it meant God was near to me and was hearing my pleas for him.

Years later, when nearly all of this stopped, I went to the Holy Land, in Jerusalem. I went inside a church called the Church of the Holy Sepulcher where Jesus was laid to rest in his tomb after he was crucified, and I touched the stone where he was laid upon. After touching the stone slab, I looked up in the dome of the church where three white doves were hovering just above me. That was awesome. I'll never forget that moment of being near Jesus where he once rested and seeing a representation of the Holy Spirit high above me.

On the other hand, the evil also had its sign, that of the vultures flying overhead, perching onto a dying tree like the time when about fifty vultures lit into a tree near my weekend home and wouldn't leave even when I took shots with my shotgun to run them off. They would not leave me alone, and it made me feel awful. Sometimes, the evil leaves dead worms on the ground for me to walk by and to think that I must be a worm and death was going to happen to me. At other times, I would walk by dead grasshoppers to remind me of what my destiny would be like.

During this ordeal, I had no one to talk with except my psychiatrist and my wife, but they didn't believe what I was going through was spiritual but rather they thought may have lost my mind. I yearned for someone to talk to, who would believe in me, and not think me touched. I told the Lord, at least you had twelve who believed in you, I had none and I needed some support to go on. I prayed for someone to hear me and understand me. Well, soon after, I prayed for help. I went to the Charismatic Center for Mass. I really prayed hard for help and after Mass, I walked up to a strange lady and began to tell her my plight with evil. She listened to every word and said she understood me and that my plight was all right for it was coming from the Lord himself and his might. I was elated that she believed in me like no other even if she was a stranger. I thanked her, hugged her and even loved her; I wondered what her name was but failed to ask, but then, I looked down at her nametag and her name was none other than "Mary." When I saw this, I came unglued because her name was none other than the Virgin Mary who was in the bible who bore God's Son and took care of him just as the lady Mary in church had taken care of me by believing in me and supporting me to go on till the end. The Blessed Virgin Mary would be my heavenly mother too, till the final chapter is over and when it is, I want the Virgin Mary to be there by my side like the lady Mary who was at the Center that glorious day. Praise be to God.

On another day, I was at Sunday Mass at the Charismatic Church with my wife and it was time for the Holy Communion part of the Mass to start when the priest changes bread and wine into Christ's Body and Blood. Standing up on the wall behind the altar was a huge 8 ft x 8ft painting of "The Risen Christ" facing me and holding out his arms to expose his wounds on them and in a loving and caring position to express his love for me. The painting caught my attention while the priest was praying to make the transubstantiation of bread and wine into the Body and Blood of Jesus. A powerful love for Jesus overcame me while looking at his picture, and I could feel his awesome love and I closed my eyes to feel his love even more. When I did this, the blackness in my eyes from being closed became lit up with a vision of Jesus in a dazzling white robe facing a snow-white altar with two angels, with wings spread high, on the right side of the altar facing Jesus. Then I noticed a white cloth covered object on the altar in front of Jesus. I watched Jesus take from under the cloth cover, a golden chalice with windows showing through so you could see the fruit of the vine. He pulled the chalice out from under the cloth, lifted it up with his hands and drank all of the wine, which was his blood that was poured out for us. I knew instantly this was THE LORD for he had no face and as he said to Moses in Ex. 33:20, "You cannot see my face for no one may see me and live." This was not all, the vision panned down to below the altar where there were eighteen to twenty-four souls standing as if dead wearing hooded dull white robes. The next vision was a rider-less white horse flying or running by and then a huge half of a wooden cross, then another golden small cross went by. Things went black for a moment. I waited for more and all of a sudden, there appeared a huge flying saucer-like image float by, turning clock-wise very slowly and it was all lit up with many colors moving through the circular object as it turned around on its axis. The object had thousands of honey-comb like cells or eyes within it. And there above it was the small golden cross on top of the object, turning around slowly. At the time, I had no idea what the visions stood for and it didn't matter to me what they were. I just wanted to bask in the glory of the Lord I saw with my own closed eyes. It was private and intimate, the evil couldn't wreck it. Much later, I came across what some of the meaning was since, some of it was in the bible and I would like to share it with you. The first image of Jesus drinking the wine can be found in the Gospel of Luke 22:17-18, which says, "After taking the cup, he gave thanks and said 'take this and divide it among you. For I tell you I will not drink again of the fruit of the vine until **the Kingdom of God comes**." I didn't rightly understand the meaning of this vision but nevertheless, I saw him drink from the fruit of the vine, which must mean the kingdom of God is upon us, if not already with us.

    The next vision of the souls under the altar can be found in Revelations 6:9-11, which says, "When he opened the fifth seal,

I saw under the altar the souls of those who had been slain because of the word of God and the testimony they had maintained. They called out in a loud voice, 'How long Sovereign Lord, holy and true, until you judge the inhabitants of the earth and avenge our blood?' Then each of them was given a white robe, and they were told to wait a little longer, until the number of fellow servants and brothers who were to be killed was completed."

The next vision of the white horse can be found in Revelations 6:1, where it says, "I watched as the Lamb opened the first seal of the seven seals. Then I heard one of the four living creatures say in a voice like thunder, 'Come.' I looked, and there before me was a white horse."

The remaining images of the crosses must be those of Jesus when he was crucified and when he rose in glory to his home above in his kingdom of heaven at the right hand of the Lord God, Almighty. I further believe the flying saucer-like image could have been the Holy City, the New Jerusalem, coming down out of heaven from God, prepared as a bride beautifully dressed for her husband, (Rev 21:2).

Now, I would like to talk more about the earth—changing so suddenly and drastically—as I found it in the bible in Revelations, which said the seven angels who had seven trumpets prepared to sound them. The first angel sounded his trumpet and there came hail and fire mixed with blood and it was hurled down upon the earth. A third of the earth was burned up, a third of the trees were burned up, and all the green grass was burned up. I didn't witness the hail, fire, and blood but I did witness a third of the earth and a third of the trees and all of the grass burned up. If you can, just try and look out around you and imagine nearly everything burned up and having the drab colors of gray, brown, and black. It was a frightful sight and a saddening one for me to see the earth in this condition. I didn't realize how colors affect one's outlook on life. The green grass, colorful trees, and flowers of life are those that bring happiness to one's soul while the drab colors of different shades of black bring sadness and depression to that soul. And sadness and depression are exactly where the evil wants us to be, so the evil can work on us to see only the negatives in life and eventually, we would either go crazy or die needlessly from suicide and fright with the anxiety in us higher than a kite. No medication given to me was capable of keeping me from being anxious and full of panic attacks.

As a survival kit, I can only suggest what I had to go through against the horror of it all and that was my unceasing prayers. I walked alone on the beach, but I wasn't alone because Jesus was with me and he must have been carrying me. I went to church and wherever I went, Jesus was with me in my heart, and I talked to him constantly. I even prayed to him unceasingly (nearly always). He touched my heart for he was my friend and I needed a friend who would believe in me, and he apparently did. To say it bluntly, we need to have a Prayer Storm down here on earth to bend God's ear and he will return our prayers with his love and care, and he will ask us to share with others, so they can also find Jesus in their hearts. Above all else, put your trust in Jesus and he will pull you through the evil's storm when and if it comes. Remember, pray unceasingly, as best you can, when the evil storm comes and you will one day take God's trip in his heavenly ship to his heavenly home high above. Above all else, don't despair, for God is there with you and you are in his loving care.

Now, I would like to quote Psalm 91 in its entirety for it best sums up what I was going through with the evil near me. It goes like this:

> He who dwells in the shelter of the Most High
> Will rest in the shadow of the Almighty.
> I will say of the Lord, "He is my refuge and my fortress,
> My God in whom I trust."
> Surely he will save you from the fowler's snare
> And from the deadly pestilence.
> He will cover you with his feathers, and under his wings
> You will find refuge; his faithfulness will be your shield
>   and rampart.
> You will not fear the terror of the night,
> Nor the arrow that flies by day,
> Nor the pestilence that stalks in the darkness,
> Nor the plague that destroys at midday.
> A thousand may fall at your side

Ten thousand at your right hand,
But it will not come near you.
You will only observe with your eyes
And see the punishment of the wicked.
If you make the Most High your dwelling
Even the Lord who is my refuge
Then no harm will befall you.
No disaster will come near your tent
For he will command his angels concerning you
To guard you in all your ways.
They will lift you up in their hands
So that you will not strike your foot against a stone
"Because he loves me," says the Lord, "I will rescue him."
I will protect him for he recognizes my name.
He will call upon me and I will answer him
I will be with him in trouble,
I will deliver him and honor him
With long life shall I satisfy him
And show him my salvation.

My depression finally lifted on July 5, 1989. I went back to work and it helped me a lot for I felt good about myself once again. Work was a positive influence on me. My company took me back after having been on short term disability for five months while I was going through this evil mess and horrible depression.

I'll never forget the time we didn't have any flags in the front of our building. I wrote a note to a higher up and within two weeks, we had an American and Texas flag brilliantly flying in front of our building. We even got around to praying around the flag early in the morning.

However, at work, whenever I would look at a blank piece of white paper, evil drawings would appear on the paper. The longer I looked at it, the more evil I saw. I couldn't look at blank paper anymore. Also, at work, I was talking to a co-worker friend and as he talked, all he could talk about was positive statements for five minutes and then negative statements for the next five. This went on for about thirty minutes, back and forth and it almost made me lose my mind. I had to excuse myself and leave him while he was rambling, on and on. What a mind binder that was. Nearly, everyday at work on my lunch hour, I would go walking near a creek that passed by near my office. As I walked, I prayed my rosary and divine mercy prayers. On one occasion right in the path that I had made from my daily walking, stood a huge bronze statue of a beast with iron jaws almost 40' high. I couldn't believe what I was seeing in front of me. It didn't move for if it did, I would have ran like crazy. Much later, I found such vision of a bronze statue in my bible. It had to do with King Nebuchadnezzar and a dream he had, and the prophet Daniel who interpreted the dream. The beast stood for a kingdom, which would come and rule over the whole earth.

It was at this point that evil came into my world even more intensely with Satan staring me in the face and trying to make my mind go unwind. He came with his multitudes of evil-looking people, even children among them, which I didn't understand. They were everywhere I went, and if they could, they would have done me in, I'm certain. Something held them in check, so all they could do was scare the living bajeebes out of me.

At times, long processions of cars all dented and in need of paint, or processions of funny cars, would drive by my house like a long funeral procession.

They kept coming and coming and would not stop. I would have to run inside to get away from this mind-bending attack. While driving my car, their cars would pull up beside mine and in front of my car and then they would all slow down to a crawl. Sometimes, I would slip away from them, but often, I couldn't get away. When I got stalled in heavy traffic they caused, I would begin to pray unceasingly and try to look the other way. Very often, this would do the trick and I could go on and drive at a normal pace. However, sometimes, I had to look at the sun while praying and this was difficult since I needed to see where I was going so as not to have a wreck or run off the road.

A good part of my world looked like a war had happened. A third of the trees and all of the grass were dead and my world had become frightening to say the least. It didn't help to see an army of evil coming my way in order to make me lose my mind. It was frightening as they projected death and devastation wherever they went. Even some of the buildings were blackened and in need of paint. Death signs were everywhere. Like them wearing tee shirts with R.I.P. on them reminding me of my upcoming death and rest in peace.

On one occasion only, the evil spoke to me while I was walking by him. He shouted at me, "Help me, help me. It's all squares in here and I can't get out." This was frightening to me for the evil never spoke to me, before or after, and I was reminded of the red squares on the wall during my first vision of hell.

I had a hard time dealing with the evil for the evil was cunning and smart, and could and would do most anything to bring me to my knees, trying to pull me away from my dear sweet Lord and Savior who topped all the evil could muster up.

Of all the things the evil did, this was no comparison of what God can do. God was God and he was not limited to anything. He did it all and eventually took charge of my dilemma and caused it all to gradually go back where it came from and my mind became at peace once again. I believe this happened when I gave up praying so much for I was worn out from it all.

I needed a rest so I went to my weekend hide away in the East Texas piney woods to try and get as close to God as I could. I decided to make a tape recording of Holy Scriptures to the background of classical music. Every move I made in reading the scriptures ended at the end of each classical song. It was breathtaking and awesome and I could feel the power of God Almighty reverberating throughout the tape. I named it from Christmas to Easter. I made three copies and gave them all to various priests who I thought should have them. There was one priest who was my elementary school priest and he asked me when I was young to play quarterback on his football team. I let him down with a stern "No." And again, he asked me would I be president of a youth club. I turned him down again for my answer was "No." I just didn't want the responsibility at that time. So now, I caught him driving up to me on his church grounds as I was delivering the tape to him, and I gave it to him and told him, "This time, I will not let you down. This is the best I can give you so enjoy." Years ago, when I was young, he often played classical music and really got into it. I hope this tape topped all of his tapes. I knew it would for God himself helped me make them. The priest died soon after I gave him the tape and I never got his feedback. I had foolishly given all the tapes away and I had nothing left, including the original tape. My only hope is that the good priest passed this tape to his higher ups and they made copies for all the priests at the Seminary. The tape was that good.

On another occasion, there were some more good that happened. My mother, my wife, and I were sitting at the kitchen table one evening and my mother from out of the clear blue asked boldly, "I wonder what color Jesus' eyes were." My wife blurted out immediately, "He had blue eyes," and she hastened to excuse herself and went upstairs to the bathroom where she experienced the walls turning pink. She walked into the bedroom and they turned pink there too. All she could say was the love of Jesus was everywhere around her. She was truly blessed by this occurrence.

Chapter Four

The Gospel of Life

Now then, during my ordeal with depression, I had been helped by my Lord for it went away and I became so appreciative that I began to pray to my Lord, "Thank you, Lord, thank you. Now what can I do for you Lord, if anything? I want to do your will, not mine, so please let me know what I can do for you."

Well, it didn't take very long for me to find out what his will for me was. I was driving out of the churchyard the next Sunday when I saw a man with a sign about abortion. I asked, "Why are you so far away from where the people would be coming out of church?" He told me he wasn't allowed to protest on the church grounds, so he was out by the street. I asked him where the abortions were going on, and he told me. The next day, I drove to an abortion clinic to see for myself what was happening there. Many were praying while some were trying to interview people arriving at the clinic to talk them out of an abortion. I couldn't stay more than an hour for I quickly felt very sad in my heart for I could see two people going in, but only one coming out. Something inside me welled up and made me cry for the children were dying and the police were there to protect the abortionist of all things instead of the tiny children. I wondered what had happened to our country to allow such an evil as abortion to procreate itself and our laws were supporting and protecting it. I drove home in dismay from where the babies were being put to death.

The next Saturday, I went back to the abortion clinic to pray again since I had no practice as an interviewer on such an important manner. I prayed and watched the other interviewers to learn from them their methods that sometimes worked. Sad to say, only a few mothers stopped long enough to hear them out. At most, the interviewer had about fifteen seconds to talk the mother out of an abortion and that just wouldn't get it. By the time the mother gets to the clinic, she is bound and determined to go through with the abortion and her boyfriend or husband are stalking her to go through with it. I managed to go to the clinic and began interviewing a little. It was so depressing to watch them go through to the parking area and get out and walk into the clinic where death and destruction were practiced by someone called an abortionist. Once in a while, an interviewer got the mother's attention long enough for her to try and talk her out of the abortion. With glee sometimes—but seldom—it worked and all would cheer with happiness. Even I, once talked a mother out of an abortion, for sure because she later called me and thanked me for she already had her baby. She told me it was a girl and she would be going to college with her child by her side. I felt if only one were saved by my efforts, it was worthwhile to spend that time at the clinic. As time went on, I began to despair because so few mothers changed their minds. I decided there must be a better way to save all of the babies, not just a few, so I began to write letters to the highest levels. To date, I had over many written with no meaningful response from any of them. Meanwhile, I heard that fifty million babies have lost their lives to abortion in America since the infamous Roe case in '73. Writing these letters have taught me a lot for I have scanned the bible for some word from God and I have found such passages that dealt with pregnant mothers who have been hit by an offender (the abortionist) and they lose their baby. The passage is Exodus 21:22-25, which I quote:

"If men who are fighting hit a pregnant woman and she gives birth prematurely but there is no serious

> injury, the offender must be fined whatever the husband demands and the court allows. But if there is 'serious injury,' you are to take <u>life for life,</u> eye for eye, tooth for tooth, hand for hand, foot for foot, wound for wound, burn for burn, bruise for bruise."

This equates to the same thing as what an abortionist does when he punctures the brain of a fetus and sucks out its blood and brains, leaving it dead to be discarded somehow. I don't know how the aborted babies are discarded. Who knows?

Another passage says in Genesis 9:5-6, "And for your lifeblood I will surely demand an accounting…and from each man too, I will demand an accounting for the life of his fellow man. Whoever sheds the blood of man, by man shall his blood be shed; for in the image of God has God made man."

Still, another passage says in 1 Corinthians 3:16-17, "Don't you know that you yourselves are God's temple and that God's Spirit lives in you? If anyone destroys God's temple, God will destroy him; for God's temple is sacred, and you (and the unborn) are that temple.

And another in Ezekiel 16:20-23, "And you took your sons and daughters whom you bore to me and sacrificed them as food to the idols…you slaughtered my children and sacrificed them to the idols. In all your detestable practices…you did not remember the days of your youth, when you were naked and bare, kicking about in your blood. Woe to you declares the Lord."

And another Isaiah 44:24, "This is what the Lord says, your Redeemer, who formed you in the womb; I am the Lord, who has made all things."

And another in Isaiah 43:6-7, "Bring my sons from afar and my daughters from the ends of the earth…whom I created for my glory, whom I formed and made."

Still, another in Isaiah 46:3-4, "Listen to me…you whom I have upheld since you were conceived, and have carried since your birth. Even to your old age and gray hairs, I am he, I am he who will sustain you and I will carry you; I will sustain you and rescue you."

Moreover, in Isaiah 49:15-16, "Can a mother forget the baby at her breast and have no compassion on the child she has borne? Though she may forget, I will not forget you! See, I have engraved you on the palms of my hands; your walls are ever before me."

Also, Psalm 139:13-15, "For you created my inmost being; you knit me together in my mother's womb. I praise you for I am fearfully and wonderfully made; your works are wonderful I know that full well. My frame was not hidden from you when I was made in the secret place."

And finally, Jeremiah 1:4-5, "The word of the Lord came to me, saying, "Before I formed you in the womb I knew you, before you were born I set you apart; I appointed you as a prophet to the nations."

These are tiny persons in the womb who didn't ask to be there, but are, and each should be protected by a Constitutional Amendment, which should protect all persons, both in and out of the womb. Each and every fetus in the womb is a tiny person and no thin layer of a mother's skin can prevent it from being human. What comes out is not a dog or a frog or a hog. It's simply a young and special human being and that person can be seen vividly on an ultrasound picture. It can even show the details of the infant's face and can show its gender. At the very least in the interim, there should be a law that would require all mothers to get an ultrasound at least ten days before an abortion could be gotten and the mother should be required to name the baby at the time of the ultrasound. This would allow some bonding to take place between mother and child and perhaps, fewer abortions would occur.

On the following page is a picture of an unborn child, probably in the early stages of the third trimester. Please note the detail of a well-formed baby i.e. eyes, ears, nose, mouth, fingers, and toes. This is not the picture of some uterine waste material or some dog frog or hog. No, this is what dies in the womb, **a human little baby** each time there is an abortion. What you see is what you get and it should never be what you don't get by virtue of an abortion.

THE GOSPEL OF BILL

This child should not die for any reason why.

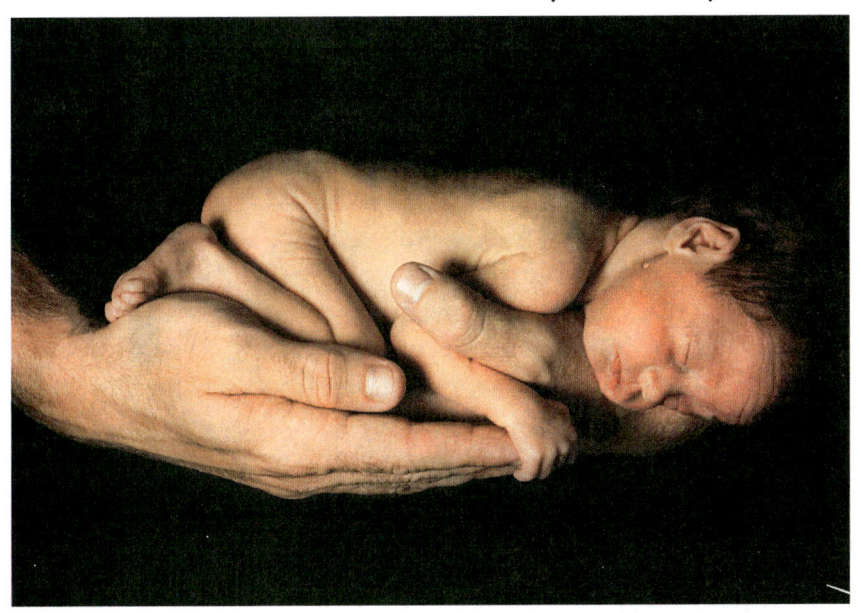

"If two men who are fighting hit a pregnant woman and she gives birth prematurely but there is no serious injury, the offender must be fined whatever the women's husband demands and the court allows. But if there is serious injury, you are to **Take Life For Life**, eye for eye, tooth for tooth, hand for hand, foot for foot, burn for burn, wound for wound, bruise for bruise." Exodus 21:22-25.

**SEE I HAVE ENGRAVED YOU
ON THE PALMS OF MY HANDS
GOD ALMIGHTY**

The Supreme Court in '73 saw to it that abortion should be legalized and they made the biggest blunder in world history, for all times, for all people, and for all places, by voting for women's choice or death to the unborn instead of GOD'S CHOICE OR LIFE for the unborn period. I wonder if we are making the next biggest blunder by not stopping abortion dead in its tracts. I ask how long is our God going to put up with such destruction for this has the potential of being the abomination of all abominations on the face of his earth. God, the Father made each of us in his image and likeness and he didn't make us for us to be aborted but rather to live a life, and one day, hopefully be able to share that life in heaven with him.

Abortion may just be the abomination or sacrifice that will cause desolation. I feel God is putting us to the test with abortions and we are failing terribly for we look the other way and say it's okay for the babies to be put away every day. The final blow may be his next show if we don't stop abortions. At the very least we all can do is start to pray for them to go away today. I promise the world is not ready to see the evil I saw in my eyes. For God's sake and the world's sake, we must get the masses to go to many Masses and pray all day for abortions to go away. If we don't, our world may end and evil will have a win and God might say I could have helped them if only they would have prayed. I feel God is willing to end this woe and come to our rescue, and if we all ask him, he will put on quite a show. He will come out and shout it out, "Evil, go out for I am now in the bout fighting with my angels and saints, and the masses in heaven and on earth will take evil out, and God will win in the end without a doubt, if only the masses on earth begin to shout it out, no more abortions, no more abortions, God's will be done."

Pro-Life Prayer of John Paul II

"Oh Mary
We entrust to you
The cause of life
Look down upon
The vast numbers
Of babies
Not allowed to be born.
Grant all who believe
In your Son
To proclaim
THE GOSPEL OF LIFE
Obtain for them the grace
To accept that Gospel
As a gift ever new,
To bear witness to it resolutely,
To the praise and glory of God,
The Creator and Lover of Life. Amen."

I had a vision. In my vision, all of the unborn would be born; Congress would pass a bill from the hill guaranteeing life for all of the unborn; the president would sign the unborn bill into law; the Supreme Court would stand up for GOD'S CHOICE of life for the unborn.

The unborn law could never be reversed; the world would follow suit; and God would say job well done for the unborn and the End Times could be born at a later date rather than sooner. But if we keep allowing the killing of the unborn, the world may be put to mourn and we may be put to scorn sooner than we would like.

God has spoken in my heart. We need a fresh start and none of the unborn should part from life either in or out of the womb. The womb should not become a temple of doom and death, but rather a sacred temple of life without any strife, where God Almighty can form his creations just as he did with each one of us who are still living today in his light. Let's don't turn out his light by aborting his delight and us winding up in the night without any light, oh what a sight, oh what a plight.

May we all stand up and thank our mothers for following God Almighty and not aborting us. Thank you, Mom and God Almighty, for giving me my life.

There is one question we should all ask ourselves and that is, what would we have done if Jesus had been aborted? To put it bluntly, there would have been no redemption and no salvation for any of us. Abortion may have killed other potentially great people who could have made a better world for us. We will never know our loss from the tragedy of abortion.

Abortion is wrong, Dead wrong and it is not all right with God. The woman's choice has got to become God's choice and that choice is the Gospel of Life. Amen!

Chapter Five

More on Good and Evil

There is a war between heaven and hell, good and evil, against the righteous and the unrighteous, and the evil is winning here on earth. It's a slam-dunk for the evil one because the good is not even in the game, but we are sitting on the sidelines looking the other way in La La land. This war is beyond us winning, since there are so few players fighting the battle for the good, but hardly anyone is praying to God for his help, and they should. God can help us win the war of all wars in the heavenly realms, as well as in the earthly realms. It just may be time to put on the full armor of God so we can take a stand against the devil's schemes. For our struggle is not against flesh and blood, but against the rulers, against the authorities, against the powers of this dark world, and against the spiritual forces of evil in both the heavenly and earthly realms. Therefore, we must put on the full armor of God so when the day of evil comes, we may be able to stand our ground.

No one knows when the end times will come except our God the Father in heaven, but **they will come.** Jesus said there would be signs in the sun, moon, and stars. When it comes, the nations of the earth will be in anguish and perplexity. Men will faint with terror, apprehensive of what is coming on the world, for the heavenly bodies will be shaken. At that time, they will see the Son of

Man coming in a cloud with power and great glory. When these things take place, stand up and lift up your heads because your redemption is drawing near. Be careful or your hearts will be weighed down with dissipation, drunkenness, and anxieties of life, and that day will close upon you like a trap for it will come upon all of those who live on the face of the earth. I have experienced the drunkenness without drinking and the anxiety associated with the evil and it is beyond horror. Without God's help, I wouldn't have made it. Now then, be always on the watch and pray that you might be able to escape all that is about to happen, and that you may be able to stand before the Son of God with his sheep who are the righteous, who will stand on his right side, and be saved for they did the good deeds like feeding the hungry, giving drink to the thirsty, clothing the naked, visiting those in prison, and tending to the sick and beyond. The Son of God will then gather the goats or unrighteous, on his left and say to them, "Depart from me, you who are cursed, go into the eternal fire prepared for the devil and his angels. For I was hungry and you didn't feed me, I was thirsty, and you did not give me drink, I was naked and you did not clothe me, and I was in prison and you didn't come visit me. Then they will go away to eternal punishment while the righteous to eternal life."

During this evil attack, I had to do whatever I had to do to keep from going crazy. I would say the Hail Marys in rapid succession over and over and over again and usually looking up to the heavens to keep from seeing the horror around me here on earth. If I hadn't done this, I would have tanked and so I thanked God and I thanked Mary for keeping me from falling into the tank with the evil ones. There are MANY who think it's wrong to pray to Mary but MANY wasn't around when I was being driven to the ground.

I did what my heart said to do and I was glad, thank you, and Jesus I feel certain was glad, too. If Mary wasn't so important, the bible wouldn't have mentioned her so much and she wouldn't be the woman who faces the dragon in the end times and she wouldn't have replaced sinful Eve as our eternal and heavenly mother for she was always without sin even to her end. I don't doubt she now must occupy her throne near her Son's throne in

God's heavenly home. I dare say Jesus might just ask, "Why didn't you pray to my mother and your heavenly Mother? She could have done a lot for you for she would have brought you to me and I could then bring you to our God the Father in heaven?" Her prayer goes like this:

Hail Mary, full of grace, the Lord is with thee, blessed are thou among women and blessed is the fruit of thy womb, Jesus.
Holy Mary, Mother of God pray for us sinners now and at the hour of our death. Amen!

I have written a poem about Mary's assumption into heaven, and I would like to share it with you.

The Assumption of Mary

Ave Maria, Salve Regina
Mother of God
Blessed be forever
With God's grace and favor
Thank you Maria
For mothering Jesus our Savior
One silent and holy night
Under a star so bright
Suffering and sorrowful you were
With a heart pierced with the spears
Mourning and weeping, a valley of tears
For your loves painful death
In atonement for men's sins
Doing this for Jesus and us
Oh glorious you became
At long last no pain
Assumed into heaven's mighty frame
Without a taint of shame
Then crowned in royal blue
With the twinkling of a star
Beaming with peace and joy

That's where and who you are.
Hail Mary! Hail Mary, Hail Mary
Thank you, dear heavenly mother

Your littlest loved ones down here.

Now then, I may have said this before but it's worth repeating. First of all, the sun reminded me of the enormous power of God and love from our God the Father.

The sun turned into a glowing mirror reflection of light, which was pleasing to my eyes. Instead of being eye burning it was eye soothing. Whenever I walked and prayed outside in daytime, I would look up at the sun instead of looking at all the evil around me that would bother me. The harder I prayed, the more evil came out to frighten me. This was a gut wrenching battle between good and evil, and I was helplessly and almost hopelessly in the middle. In the daylight, I kept my eyes on the sun in the sky for I knew God would never let me die if I looked him in the eye and I continued to hang on to his robe, so to speak. His power was awesome and it kept the evil from overcoming me. The best they could do was to scare me to death and I had learned by now that I was on a ride with Jesus by my side.

As well, the moon was also very special to me. I thought of it as a huge heavenly Host or Communion representing Jesus, the light of the world, and at night, it was so beautiful to me especially when it would rise above the sea. I walked in the dark, everywhere, including the beach and his loving light shown on me throughout the night, that kept me from fearing the fright in the night. Sometimes, I would look up at the moon and a bright star would be near the moon and I would swoon by pretending the star was me and I was getting closer to Jesus you see, and this was a love between me and he.

Also, the sea was always peaceful to me and it reminded me of the Holy Spirit in me. The evil never followed me in the water and I would often go in the water to pray and keep the evil away. I called this phenomenon the sun, the moon, the sea, and me.

In addition, the clouds of a huge thunderstorm would often appear to me and the awesome power of God would reverberate through the clouds and the lightning and thunder display was unbelievable for it was nothing like I had ever seen or heard before. God did not speak to me personally from the clouds, but I felt he was trying to communicate with the world he once created.

Now then, I would like to share with you what I FEEL is the most important question of our lives and that is, to ask ourselves what is the most important purpose in our lives? The answer to this question is **TO GET TO HEAVEN,** period. It matters not how important we are or how unimportant we are, if we lose our soul and don't get to heaven, we have lost it all, forevermore and nothing then can save us. In order to get to heaven, we should prepare ourselves to get to know, love, and serve God in the best ways we can. Some do this by going to church, others by reading the bible, and some by helping others or by just praying. We should do all of these things as our heart tells us to do, but we should not fool ourselves by just doing what we want to do. For its not doing what we want to do, but rather what **we ought to do**. Give a little and you will get a lot. There is the matter of grace from God, which can get us to heaven, but only if we have the faith and the faith comes by actions not just words. The action is the good deeds that God have in mind for us when he gives us the grace and we should always do what we feel is right not only in our eyes, but rather in the eyes of God. We all should be baptized and kept holy on the Sabbath by going to mass for Catholics or to Church services for Non-Catholics. What is good for one is good for the other and we are all in this together and we should get along with each other. Personally, I found Jesus in church, on my knees, under his cross, and in receiving Holy Communion as often as possible. I later experienced him while parking on the beach and watching the sunrise come up with some music playing on my car radio. I also found him in looking at each baby for the babies are the most important persons in God's Kingdom. These are the greatest in his kingdom, not the most important people here on earth who think they are. A baby clings to his or her mother and father, but God clings to the baby and his heart is full of love for what he made. Nothing is more beautiful then the smiling of an innocent infant while looking at you. No art, no music, no nothing compares to God's finest handiwork, the baby, and that's why he or she should not be aborted, including rape or incest, but only to save the physical life of the mother. After all, all pregnancies involve the life of a baby. These babies should be protected and can be adopted to loving parents who will love, cherish, and teach them how to get to heaven for their purpose is the same as our purpose, to get to heaven. Amen.

God said, "It is easier for a camel to go through the eye of a needle then for a rich man to get to heaven." This is because when a man gets rich, his objective is to make even more money or hang on to what he has. This is the time that is poorly spent for you can't be obsessed with one and serve the other. I am sure there are many with riches who get to heaven, but it's probably harder for them for they are contented with their station in life and may not see the need for God. You have to be hungry to go out and get the game. If you are always satisfied, there is no need to hunt. We should be hungry for God because it's him who made us, and him who watches over us, and him who cares the most for us, and him who can bring us to eternal life in Heaven. And we should care about each other for everyone is made in God's image and likeness and he loves all of us, especially the littlest babies who should never be aborted except to save the physical life of the mother

As powerful as the devil was in this unusual war between good and evil, he was no match for the power of God. He put on a good show but in the end, God made him go and he was never in control but he was creative in his antics against me. Almost nothing was left unimagined and he was clever and cunning. The evil wasn't always like a ghost or scary monster people for some of them looked as normal as you and I. I knew evil by their actions when I saw them and they tried to make me go insane with their antics. However, they were no match for God's ingenuity, for he was totally awesome without limitations to what he could do and he did all that was necessary to bring me back home again. I was totally frightened at times, but I knew I was walking and talking with the Almighty Himself and I didn't need to worry. **How great thou art.**

There once was a comedian whose slogan was, "The devil made me do it." Well, this was a true saying, for the devil did make me do it for he brought me even closer to God than I could ever have been before. The devil was so powerful that I needed something even more powerful and I found it in God Almighty.

I would like to say here that all of the evil vanished when I told the Lord I could pray no more for I could take no more of this monumental event. I think, the Lord was waiting for this request for he promptly ended it over a short time and all became normal to me again, except for one thing, I always continue to try and stay close to My Lord and Savior who is in control of everything including me and I continue to pray and go to church a lot, even today. I just don't want to go back the other way skipping church and ignoring God who made me and who has a place in heaven for me. I love him too much to ignore him now and I know what the alternatives are, the devil and his crew who are always blue. Amen!

Finally, one of the other good things I saw either in visions or dreams was the sea of emerald green water like crystal, with a throne standing in the middle of it. Another was St. Peter in the clouds on his cross turning upside down. Still, another was a beautiful garden with two white marble columns in it. There were more good things but twenty years have dulled my memory a bit. I wished I had kept a diary but I didn't have time to write in it for so much was happening to me both day and night, keeping me in a state of fright.

Chapter Six

Holy Scriptures

Now, I would like to quote from Scriptures where the Holy Spirit led me too, in God's Bible, His Book of Love. They are not in any particular order and they deal with the love of God for us, with the evil within and around us, and the good that God wants for us. There are not all of the most important quotes but they are important and are a good sampling of what God has in mind for us:

In the beginning, God created the heavens and the earth and everything in it. God created man in his own image, in the image of God he created him: male and female he created them. God saw everything he had made and it was very good. God blessed them and said to them, "Be fruitful and multiply." The Lord God formed man from the dust of the ground and breathed into his nostrils the breath of life, and the man became a living being. The Lord God said, "It is not good for man to be alone. I will make a helper suitable for him." The Lord God caused the man to fall into a deep sleep; and while he was sleeping he took one of the man's ribs and closed up the place with flesh. Then the Lord God made a woman from the rib taken out of man and he brought her to the man. For this reason, a man will leave his father and mother and be united to his wife and they will become one flesh. Nobody, including God has been satisfied with human beings, since then.

We were made to be very good but we disobeyed God right from the beginning. We've been suffering the consequences ever since. The universe is so fragrantly lovely, and yet so tragic. It is lovely because God made it out of his love for us but it is tragic because he trusted it to us, and we failed, and the evil then spread throughout the earth even till this very day, (Gen. 1, 2 and 3).

Out of love, God made each one of us for them to know, love, and serve him. He will provide for us everything we need to get to heaven. God must have said, "Can a mother forget her baby at her breast and have no compassion for the child she has borne. Though she may forget, I will not forget you. See I have engraved you on the palms of my hands; your walls are ever before me," (Isa. 49:15-16).

"But if a wicked man turns away from all of his sins he has committed and keeps all my decrees and does what is just and right, he will surely live; he will not die. None of his offences he had committed will be remembered against him. Because of the righteous things he has done, he will live," (Ezek. 18:21).

Now, when he saw the crowds, Jesus went up on a mountainside and sat down. His disciples came to him and he began to teach them saying, "Blessed are the poor in spirit, for theirs is the kingdom of heaven. Blessed are they who mourn for they will be comforted. Blessed are the meek, for they will inherit the earth. Blessed are they who hunger and thirst for righteousness for they will be filled. Blessed are the merciful, for they shall be shown mercy.

Blessed are the pure in heart for they will see God. Blessed are the peacemakers for they will be called sons of God. Blessed are those who are persecuted because of righteousness, for theirs is the kingdom of heaven. Blessed are you when people insult you, persecute you and falsely say all kinds of evil against you because of me.. Rejoice and be glad because great is your reward in heaven for in the same way they persecuted the prophets who were before you," (Matt. 5:1-12).

"Do not judge, or you will be judged," (Matt. 7:1).

"Ask and it will be given to you, Seek and you will find; knock and the door will be opened to you. For everyone who asks receives; he who seeks finds and to him who knocks the door will be opened to you," (Matt. 7:7).

"Jesus called a little child and had him stand among them. And he said 'I tell you the truth unless you change and become like little children, you will never enter the kingdom of heaven.' Therefore, who humbles himself likes this child is the greatest in the kingdom of heaven and whoever welcomes a child like this in my name welcomes me," (Matt. 18:2-5). Are we welcoming his unborn children.

For as lightning comes from the east is visible even in the west, so will be the coming of the Son of Man. Wherever there is a caucass, there the vultures will gather. Immediately after the distress of those days, the sun will be darkened and the moon will not give its light, the stars will fall from the sky, and the heavenly bodies will be shaken. At that time, the sign of the Son of Man will appear in the sky and all the nations of the earth will mourn. They will see the Son of Man coming on the clouds of the sky, with power and great glory Mat. 24:27-31

"This is the verdict. Light has come into the world, but men loved darkness instead of light, because of their evil. Everyone who does evil hates the light for fear that his deeds will be exposed. But whoever lives by the truth comes into the light, so that it may be seen plainly that what he has done has been done through God," (John 3:19-20).

Moreover, the Father judges no one but has entrusted all judgment to the Son, that all may honor the Son just as they honor the Father. He, who does not honor the Son, does not honor the Father, (John 5:22-23). Jesus said to them, "I tell you the truth, unless you eat the flesh of the Son of Man and drink his blood, you have no life in you. Whoever eats my flesh and drinks my blood has eternal life, and I will raise him up on the last day. For my flesh is real food and my blood is real drink. Whoever eats my flesh and drinks my blood remains in me and I in him," (John 6:53–57).

Jesus answered, "I am the way and the truth and the life. No one comes to the Father except through me," (John 14:6).

Jesus replied, "Love the Lord your God with all your heart, and with all your soul and with all your mind. This is the first and greatest commandment. And the second is like it Love your neighbor as yourself. All the Law and the Prophets hang on these two Commandments," (Matt. 22:37–40).

Jesus replied, "If anyone loves me, he will obey my teaching. My father will love him and we will come down and make our home with him," (John 14:23).

"Greater love has no one than this that he lay down his life for his friends. You are my friends if you do what I command. I no longer call you servants because a servant doesn't know his master's business. Instead I call you friends, for everything I learned from my Father, I have made known to you.

You did not choose me, but I chose you and appointed you to go and bear fruit, fruit that will last. Then the Father will give you whatever you ask in my name. This is my command: Love each other," (John 15:13-17).

"If anyone does not provide for his relatives and especially for his immediate family, he has denied the faith and is worse than an unbeliever," (1 Tim. 5:8).

Near the cross of Jesus stood his mother, his mother's sister, Mary, the wife of Clopas, and Mary Magdalene. When Jesus saw his mother there and the disciple whom he loved, standing nearby, he said to his mother, 'Dear Woman, here is your son," and to the disciple, "here is your mother.' From that time on the disciple took her into his home," (John 19:25-27).

"Rejoice in the Lord always. I will say it again. Rejoice! Let your gentleness be evident to all. The Lord is near. Do not be anxious about anything, but in everything by prayer and petition with thanksgiving, present your request to God. And the peace of God, which transcends all understanding, will guard your hearts and your minds in Christ Jesus," (Phil. 4:4-9).

"Since then, you have been raised with Christ; set your heart on the things above, where Christ is seated at the right hand of God. Set your minds on things above, not on earthly things," (Col. 3:1-4).

"There, as God's chosen people, holy and dearly loved, clothe your self with compassion, kindness, humility, gentleness, and patience. Bear with each other and forgive whatever grievances you may have against each other. Forgive as the Lord forgave you.

And over all of these virtues put on love, which binds them together in perfect unity," (Col 3:1-4).

"Endure hardship like a good soldier of Christ Jesus. The Lord will rescue me from every evil attack and will bring me safely to his heavenly kingdom. To him, be glory forever and ever, Amen. Alleluia!"(2 Tim. 2:3).

"So do not throw away your confidence; it will be richly rewarded. You need to persevere so that when you have done the will of God, you will receive what he has promised. For in just a very little while, 'He who is coming will come and not delay. But my righteous one will love by faith. And if he shrinks back I will not be pleased with him," (Heb. 10:35–39).

"And without faith it is impossible to please God, because anyone who comes to him must believe that he exists and that he rewards those who earnestly seek him," (Heb. 11:6).

"Blessed is the man who perseveres under trial, because when he has stood the test, he will receive the crown of life that God promised to those who love him," (Jas. 1:12).

"Faith by itself if it is not accompanied by action is dead," (Jas. 2:7).

"<u>God opposes the proud</u> but gives grace to the humble. Submit yourselves then to God. Resist the devil, and he will flee from you. Come near to God and he will come near to you. Humble yourselves before the Lord and he will lift you up," (Jas. 4:6–8).

"Therefore, since God has suffered in his body, arm yourself also with the same attitude, because he who has suffered in his body is done with sin. As a result, he does not live the rest of his earthly life for evil human desires, but rather for the will of God," (1Pet. 4:1-2).

"Dear friends, do not be surprised at the painful trial you are suffering, as though something strange were happening to you. But rejoice that **you participate in the sufferings of Christ** so that you may be overjoyed when his glory is revealed," (1Pet. 4:12-13).

"Humble yourselves, therefore, under God's mighty hand, that he may lift you up in due time. Cast all your anxiety on him because he cares for you. Be self controlled and alert. Your enemy the devil prowls around like a roaring lion looking for someone to devour. Resist him, standing firm in your faith. And the God of all grace, who called you to his eternal glory in Christ, after you have suffered a little while, will himself restore you and make you strong. To him, be the power forever and forever. Amen!" (1 Pet. 5:6-11).

"No one who is born of God will continue to sin, because he has been born of God. This is how we know who the children of God are and who the children of the devil are. Anyone who does not do what is right is not a child of God." (1John 3:9-10).

"There is no fear in love, but perfect love drives out all fear because fear has to do with punishment. The one who fears is not made perfect in love," (1John 4:18).

"Everyone who believes that Jesus is the Christ is born of God, and everyone who loves the Father, loves his child as well. This is how we love the children of God by loving God and carrying out his commands. This is love for God to obey his commands. And his commands are not burdensome for everyone born of God overcomes the world. This is the victory that has overcome the world, even our faith. Who is it that overcomes the world? Only he who believes that Jesus is the Son of God," (1 John 5:1–5).

"We know that anyone who is born of God does not continue to sin; the one who was born of God, God keeps him safe, and the evil one cannot harm him. We know that we are children of God and that the whole world is in control by the evil one," (1 Jn 5:18–19).

"Blessed are those who wash their robes, that they may have the right to the tree of life and may go into the gates through the city. Outside are the dogs, those who practice magic arts, the sexually immoral, the murderers, the idolaters and everyone who practices falsehood," (Rev. 22:14–15).

"Jesus said that I have told you these things, so that in me you may have peace. In this world you will have trouble. But take heart, I have overcome the world," (John 16:33)

"Holy Father, protect them by the power of your name, the name you gave me," (John 17:11). (Jesus)

"At that time, there will be signs in the sun moon and stars. On the earth nations will be in anguish and perplexity at the roaring and tossing of the sea. Men will faint from terror, apprehensive of what is coming on the world, for the heavenly bodies will be shaken. At that time they will see the Son of Man coming in a cloud with power and great glory. When these things take place, stand up, and lift your heads because your redemption is drawing near," (Luke 21:25-28).

"Nation will rise against nation, kingdom against kingdom. There will be earthquakes in various places, and famines. These are the beginning of the birth pains. Such things happen but the end is still to come," (Mark 13:7-8).

"When you see the abomination that causes desolation standing where it does not belong, pray that this does not take place in winter, because those will be the days of distress unequaled from the beginning, when God created the world until now and never be equaled again," (Mark 3:14-19).

"No one knows about that day or the hour, not even the angels in heaven, nor the Son, but only the Father," (Mark 13:32-33).

"At that time, the Son of Man will appear in the sky and all the nations of the earth will mourn. They will see the Son of Man coming on the clouds of the sky in great glory," (Matt. 24:30).

"I often wonder if my vision of him on the cross in the sky all lit up is what he will look like when he comes again. It could be! In the last days your sons and daughters will prophesy, your young men will see visions," (Act 2:17).

"I am convinced that neither death nor life, neither angels nor demons, neither the present nor the future; nor any powers, neither height nor depth, not anything else in all creation will be able to separate us from the love of God that is in Christ Jesus our Lord," (Rom. 8:38–39).

Finally, "Be strong in the Lord and in his mighty power. Put on the full armor of God so that you can take your stand against the devil's schemes. For our struggle is not against flesh and blood, but against the rulers, against the authorities, against the powers of this dark world, and against the spiritual forces of evil in the heavenly realms," (Eph. 6:10–12).

Chapter Seven

Conclusion

I would like to express again the need to accomplish our mission on earth and that is to get to heaven no matter what it takes to accomplish it for that is the most important purpose in our life. To fail here means disaster to our souls. We should try our best not to sin, but if we do, we should ask God with our whole heart to forgive us. If we are Catholic, then we should go to our priest confessor and before him, ask God with all our heart to forgive us, and he will. There are some like my father who was not Catholic and who almost never went to church, but I knew he always did the right things instead of the wrong ones and hopefully he went to heaven for doing the good deeds God laid out for him. Shortly after he died, I dreamt he was on the roof of our two-story home and he began to slide off headfirst and before he hit bottom, two mighty hands grabbed him by his ankles and pulled him back, not letting him fall to the ground. I know he slipped, but I know he didn't fall to the ground for his God and our God saved him anyway and I know he must be in heaven with God Almighty.

However, play it safe, love God with all your heart, believe in God, be baptized, go to his house of prayer—the church, pray always, and thank God for everything good that happens to you in your life. I pray that none ever see the evil I saw or rather tried hard not to see for it was unnerving. I ask, my God the Son, God the Father and God the Holy Spirit that I have said nothing that is untrue or against his will. I feel certain that my experience with evil was a precursor, warning us about good and evil, war and peace, heaven and hell, and the end times which may just be on us, and who knows, but only God the Father, and it will be his call only and we better watch for it before it kicks us where the sun don't shine, our butts.

Our country needs to take one giant leap backward like it was prior to the sixties when most of the families went to church frequently and were more respectful of the Lord. The norm for most of the people was to fear God and love the world less. By fearing God, I don't mean loving God. That's different. I mean to respect Him as the maker of all things and as one who made us by his spoken Word, and he can even destroy us by his very Word. Fear or respect of the lord should go hand in hand with love of the Lord and eventually, love will drive out all fear when the love of God reaches its maturity and his love is more important than anything else in the world. The thing we should really fear is evil and its potential grip on us, for make no mistake evil is out to rip us apart and destroy us forever and ever, and land us in the fiery furnace of the pits of hell for eternity.

Congress and the Supreme Court need to work together and make and uphold laws, favoring God's Rule again as he should be the mold for us to live and die by. There are too many atheist run organizations throughout our land, trying to pull us apart from our God. It's high time, the minority of atheist not be allowed to rule the majority of believers because this is a democracy—that should protect the majority. They should have no means to ruin our dreams and tell us a bunch of God-hating schemes made to drive God out of our Land. Our government was once based on faith in God and it should return to it. That's why our country was so special. Just look at the back of a one dollar bill. On the back of it, is a partial pyramid, our great nation, and an eye above with the words *Annuit Coeptis*, which means God's watchful eye is **smiling** on our undertakings. At the base of the pyramid are the Roman Numbers standing for the year 1776, when our nation was, birthed not aborted. And to the right, the eagle's eye is looking directly into God's eye for inspiration and direction. The eagle is flying high with its head—our executive branch, the wings—our legislative branch, and the tail feathers—our judicial branch of the government.

Somehow, I dare say today, God is no longer smiling on our undertakings with abortion legally running rampant like it is. It's high time some of the eagle's tail feathers or Judiciary, need to be plucked to grow new ones, ones that can soar like an eagle, instead of being like a lame duck that is stuck in the muck.

The ACLU must stand for **A** merica **C** annot **L** ive **U** nder God and it is trying to remove God from our nation and even from our one dollar bill, which states boldly "IN God We Trust." I say, without God, whom can we trust? I didn't know so much faith in God came from the one dollar bill. Our government should return to looking into God's eye with faith in him only, and we should go back to saying and meaning, One Nation Under God, again as expressed in our Pledge of Allegiance, period. Amen!

Our country, out of fear of being sued, has all but removed God from our schools and public places. The courts should recognize this and adapt to set a trap and drive that crap out of our lap. There I've said it and it feels good to say that we ought to do what is good just as we should, and we would be a lot better off if only we would. It's high time for, our country, used to be the land of dreams, but today has become a court full of schemes to wreck these dreams. Just as the evil increases, the good decreases, and as the good increases, the evil decreases. Our land once was very grand and we should now draw a line in the sand to make all of man equal in our plan and that should include all of the unborn boys and girls, who need a helping hand to save them from the abortion, man by damn.

Abortion is here to stay unless we pray it away the unborn should already be determined when we ask. "Is it a Girl or a Boy" we don't ask is it human, we know that already. God will help us end abortions, but only if most of us would go to many Masses and church services of all denominations kneel down together and pray together a **chant that is bigger than can't**, and that is, no more abortions, no more abortions, God's will be done. It's either La La land and fail or stand up for the little man and hail God's will be done for there should be no more abortion. If we don't and we continue letting our sons and daughters become a tomb in the womb, Lord help us for we are not ready for Jesus to come and judge us and he may just do it in haste.

Father Corapi of EWTN says it best, "In the end you and I will be in either heaven or hell period." This is so true. It's now up to you, what you can say and do. Just ask and put Jesus to the task and forever and ever you will last happily in His Kingdom that he has prepared for you Amen!

Now then, I would like to see America once again stand for God for its very name must have come from God as follows:

A LL
M EN
E NTER
R EDEMPTION
I N
C HRIST
A LMIGHTY

Jesus died on his cross for us, to save us from our sins so we would not be eternally lost. It is imperative for us to follow our Jesus' example by accepting our crosses, sorrows, and sufferings that may come our way each day. We can do this by praying and accepting the will of God, who just may be giving us a cross to bear so we can enter his home in Heaven, where there is no place like home. It's not the many blessings only, we have on earth that counts, but rather, the crosses we bear for our Lord Jesus Christ.

For it is written, Hebrew 12:5–7, "Do not make light of the Lord's discipline, and do not lose heart when he rebukes you, because the Lord disciplines those he loves and he punishes everyone he accepts as a son. Endure hardship as discipline. God is treating you as sons."

We must remember that he will not give us more than we can handle and he is with us always to help us along the way until we reach our home in Heaven.

Jesus said in Revelations 21:6–8, "I am the Alpha and the Omega, the Beginning and the End. To him who is thirsty, I will give drink without cost from the spring of the water of life. He who overcomes will inherit all this, and I will be his God and he will be my son. But the cowardly, the unbelieving, the vile, the murderers, the sexually immoral, those who practice magic arts, the idolaters and all liars, their place will be in the fiery lake of burning sulfur."

Jesus also said in Revelations 22:12, "Behold, I am coming soon! My reward is with me, and I will give to everyone according to **what he has done."**

Now then, **please do not look at the sun and pray, for it may very well damage your eyes**. This phenomenon only lasted while I was experiencing the evil around me. The evil is mostly gone now and I don't look at the sun anymore for it now burns when I do, so I don't.

I would like to say the evil came one day but didn't go away for several years. The only purpose I suppose for this happening to me was to drive me near to God and see to it I would do something to end abortions if I could. I have done all I know but have failed so far on the issue of abortion. This mini-book is dedicated to the fifty million aborted babies who have died since 1973 in America and those who have been aborted needlessly around the world.

Finally, if you have had an abortion, **do not despair for God is there and he will forgive you for he wants to be your friend till the end**. Please know you don't have to feel forgiven like I did due to my depression that made it almost impossible for me to feel forgiven. If you are truly sorry, surely you will be forgiven for Jesus forgives the un-forgiven and chances are, you are already forgiven because you feel the sorrow in your heart. And don't be too hard on yourself, but do turn to our Lord and Savior Jesus Christ for his love and care, and he will give it to you and you can count on him for he is your friend till the end. Oh, what a friend we have in him. Words cannot express the degree of his kindness and goodness and his caring way. There is no other like him except His Father and our Father, God the Father. To him please say,

Our Father, who art in heaven, hollowed be thy name. Thy kingdom come thy will be done on earth as it is in heaven. Give us this day our daily bread, and forgive us our trespasses as we forgive those who trespass against us. Lead us not into temptation but deliver us from evil, for thine is the kingdom and the power and the Glory forever. Amen."

I WILL
I WILL WALK GOD'S WALK AND TALK GOD'S TALK
I WILL HURT GOD'S HURT AND FEEL GOD'S FEEL
I WILL CARE GOD'S CARE AND SHARE GOD'S SHARE
I WILL LOVE GOD'S LOVE AND RIDE GOD'S RIDE
WITH JESUS BY MY SIDE.
I WILL JESUS
IF THY WILL IT TOO

No matter what you say and do
God can and will forgive you too
If you are truly blue.
It is done and it is true
Thank you ***GOD*** for being you.

Jesus sings his song to us
I love you, I love you, I love I do
I love you, I love you, I love you so true
Love lifted me, up on the cross for thee
I love you, I love you, I love you, I do
I love you, I love you, I love you so true
Love one another love each other
I love you, I love you, I love you I do
I love you, I love you, I love you so true

May this be ***GOD'S WILL***
Just Bill

The Gospel of Bill

WHAT IS THE MEANING OF THESE CROSSES?

ABORTION KILLS 154 BABIES EACH AND EVERY HOUR, AND THE CLOCK IS TICKING...
These crosses represent the innocent children whose hearts were beating, living and growing within their mother, yet this past hour each were torn from the womb and unjustly denied their RIGHT TO LIVE... Little martyrs.
Could one of these have carried the cure for Cancer, Heart Disease, Diabetes, Leukemia?? God may have chosen one to be a peacemaker, to unlock the hearts of warring nations and bring harmony. One may have had a heart like Mother Teresa, or have become a Priest or Pope, a Doctor or Nurse, Teacher, Farmer or Craftsman.

ONLY GOD KNOWS WHAT WAS IN THE GIFT THAT HE GAVE!
This hour begins a lifetime of pain and regret for the mothers and the fathers who have let their children be killed -their souls darkened by this great evil.
Don't we all share the blame? We allow this to continue with little protest! Is our SILENCE helping to promote a **Culture of Death**? We will all answer to God someday. What will *your* answer be?

LORD, IN THE NAME OF JESUS, PLEASE DELIVER US FROM THIS EVIL AND RESTORE IN US AND IN OUR LAND...
A Culture of Life

Father, Father

Father, Father, we are crying down here
Father, Father, can you hear us down here
Father, Father, we are dying down here
No one down here seems to care for us
Won't you once again send us Jesus
For no one but him can free us
From the abortion that kills us
And shortens our lives to days, not years
Father, Father, can you see our tears
Father, Father, we have so many fears
Father, Father, all we want is to have some cheers
In seeing our earthly mother and father
Father, Father, can you hear us down here
Father, Father, will you be near
Father, Father, you will be so dear
Please love us and come be with us
We will be so happy when you come to us
Knowing you came to us
And one day you will free us, free us
When the world down here prays enough
And says, "Enough is enough. No more abortion."
We need this world to end this commotion
Father, Father, God's will be done.

He Gave Us His All

Brazen men marched on him in the Garden
His disciples were with him
They didn't know what to do for him
All were scared and frightened
One at heart took a sword
And cut off the ear of one of them
Jesus said, "Wait," and put it back.
"We will not be on the attack.
Let them do what they came to do.
There will be no rescue.

"I must meet the test and do my best
For my Father in heaven is counting on me
To be the best of all his brethren.
I prayed to Him, 'Thy will be done.'
Let them come; I will not run."

They captured Him and beat Him
They shoved Him and spit on Him
They took Him away to do Him in
Pilot said, "I find no wrong with Him.
What do you want me to do?"
They said, "Crucify Him! Crucify Him!"
And they said, "Let his blood be on our head
And on our children as well."
They must have said, "He must go to hell."

They crowned Him with thorns on His head
And whipped Him till he was near dead
They gave Him a cross and He was at a loss
He fell three times in agony and pain
The cross was too heavy for him
They nailed Him and lifted Him up on a cross
To bleed him to death.

He looked up in the sky
And asked His Father, "Why must I die?"
He yelled out to Him with a cry
Jesus said, "Not my will but thy will be done."
He must have said, "You must be suffering
As much as I to see me like this up on a tree
To set them free for eternity."

He gave His life with all this strife
To lift them up out of the grave
And come be with us in heaven
As you wished He gave them His All
That's the best He could have done for us
He did his Father's will
He gave us His All for us all
Thank you, Jesus, for freeing us
To be with thee for eternity.

Jesus

Amazing grace, amazing grace, amazing grace in thee
Amazing grace, amazing grace, amazing grace in thee, oh Lord
Oh Lord, oh Lord, oh Lord our God above
Oh Lord, our God
Precious Jesus, precious Jesus, precious Jesus
Precious Jesus in us
Sweet Jesus, sweet Jesus
How sweet thou art
Sweet Jesus in our heart
Thank you, Jesus. Thank you, Jesus
For your being born for us
For your suffering and dying
On the cross for us
For your rising above
Into God's heavenly home
At the right hand of God
Is your throne.
Praise God, praise God, praise God
Praise God, praise God
Praise God, praise God
Praise God.

Sung in part to the song "Amazing Grace"

Maria

Ave Maria, Salve Regina
Mother of God
Blessed be forever
Thank you, Maria,
For mothering Jesus, our Savior
Ave, Ave, Ave Maria
Hail Mary, Hail Mary, Hail Maria
Amen. Amen.

Sung in part to the song "Ave Maria"

Mariah

Oh my love, my God above
I want you, I need you, I love you so much
I want to feel your tender touch
Will you be mine till the end of time
I want to shine, I need to shine
Let me feel your gentle wind. Mariah, Mariah
Will you take my cross from me
And give me a crown for eternity
Let me love and be with thee
With your gentle wind on me. Mariah, Mariah
Elijah, Isaiah, Nehemiah, Jeremiah
Prophets of old ever so bold
Telling God's truth for our very own soul
Let us become your nuggets of gold
And follow God's truthful role. Mariah, Mariah
We want to be like a gem
Will you please just let us in
Through your gate to heaven
We want to meet your brethren
And above the rest will be the best
Father, Son, and Holy Ghost
We want to see your Heavenly Host
We want to stay your course. Mariah, Mariah
We want to see our Heavenly Mother
In your home out yonder
Where there is peace, love, and joy without any thunder
Where the breeze is called God's gentle wind a wonder.
MARIAH, MARIAH, MARIAH.

Mommy

Mommy, I can hear you speak
From here in your womb
That's pretty neat
I need to tell you I heard the bad news
I heard the doctor say
You may not make it through another day
Don't be afraid, Mommy. Be brave
For I will give my life for you
You needn't cry a tear, so don't be blue
I'll be seeing you again, it's true
I had a purpose in dying
To give you life, so keep on trying
Maybe we will meet again
I hope I will be going straight to heaven
I hope I can get a glimpse of you
As they take me away from you
I am so glad I could save you
Have a happy life, Mommy
God loves us both, Mommy
And he has a place in heaven high above
For you and for me to be in love.
Bye bye, Mommy.

Thy Will Be Done

No more abortions, no more abortions
That's God's way for the U.S.A.
And for the whole world today
We will pray the Divine Mercy
And the Rosary each and every day
At three o'clock and around the clock
Please show us the way to a better day
Please unlock your church doors
We are coming to pray abortion away
No more abortions, no more abortions
Thy Will be done.

If we have to, we will even march to a different drum
We will come and come
One by one, one by one, for His only Son
Our dear sweet Jesus, will you come to us?
We want you, we need you, we need you now so much
We need your tender touch
No more abortions, no more abortions
In the U.S.A. and in the whole world today
Thy will be done.

We must get the notion to end all abortion
It's time to be on our knee
To pray to the Lord to set them free
They have God's right to life without any strife
Stop cutting them up with a knife
We will pray all day on our knee
To be all that they can be
We need your power high above any tower
Will you send your angels
To help us walk the walk and talk the talk?
No more abortions, no more abortions
Thy will be done.

Where Are You, My Jesus?

Where are you, my Jesus?
I'm looking for you
My heart is empty
Longing for you
When will I find you
Where will I go
Where are you, my Jesus?
I'm looking for you.

When will you come to me
I want to be with thee till eternity
I want you, I need you
I love you so much
I want to feel your tender touch
Where are you, my Jesus?
I'm looking for you.

I'll walk the sand of the beach
I want to feel your loving reach
I'm right here for you, dear Jesus
I'll be yours forevermore
Will you let me come to your shore
Where the gentle waves of the sea
Are rolling in so close to me
Bringing the Holy Spirit from thee
Where are you, my Jesus?
I'm looking for you.

Now I'm on top of your mountain
With the snow all around
As white as can be as pure as can be
It must be you I'm trying to see
My heart is aching for you
Where are you, my Jesus?
I'm looking for you.

I'm up here in heaven, waiting for you
I hear your calling
You are my darling
I'm coming to you
I'm now in your heart
I'm now in your soul
I have refined you
And you are now as pure as gold
I'll take you by my your hand
And lead you to where it's so grand
You will be a star above the rainbow
Where all of my stars want to go
I have taken your cross
And given you a crown
Now you are one of renown.

Thank you, my Jesus, for forgiving me
I now know you were with me
All of the time when I didn't shine
And now I know I will be in your light
I'll shine just right with all of my might
You are so kind all of the time
You are my Jesus and my delight. Amen!

The 185

Way back in 1836, a very long time ago
When men of spirit so brave and bold
Came from the foothills of Tennessee
To the plains of a new birthing country
They joined as brothers Crockett, Bowie, and others
To stand hand and hand against a tyrant of a man
For the common good of an infant land
They came to fight do or die at the Alamo.

For ten days or more the 185 stood their ground
Against an army numbering several thousand
And a general calling surrender or death by sword
The valiant 185 fought hard and not wanting to die
They called for help and their cry went out
Before the last great charge, they were asked at large,
"Surrender your life or death my swords, the choice is yours."
The men at war would not get help, they would stand to the end
The commander in chief lay sick and wounded with one last breath
With a shout of gut and glory, the cannon sounded and replied
The enemy's ears were branded with their cry, victory or death
The charge then came, they fought their heart till all 185 had died.

After doing them in, the generals' men tipped their hats and swords
For the 185 could not have stayed alive against the thousands odds
They knew their lives was liberty's price, that a state called Texas
Would one day be born into a mother's country arm, the U.S.A.
With this vision on their mind, they fell asleep in the arms of their Lord.

With courage and honor, the 185 marched to a different drum
They were united to fight do or die and did a job best done
The enemy thought the battle won, but the 185 who died inspired the rest
To do their best and meet the test at Sam Houston's San Jacinto
As they cried out in victory, "Remember the Alamo!"

They came, they fought, they won from the plains where longhorns roam
To the shores of Galveston, TEXAS will be our new home.